SHORT DAYS, LONG NIGHTS

Helen Dunmore was born in 1952 in Beverley, Yorkshire. After studying English at York University, she taught in Finland for two years. She is a freelance writer, and lives in Bristol.

Helen Dunmore has published four books of poems: *The Apple Fall* (1983), *The Sea Skater* (1986), *The Raw Garden* (1988), and *Short Days, Long Nights: New & Selected Poems* (1991), all published by Bloodaxe Books. She won the Alice Hunt Bartlett Award for *The Sea Skater* in 1987. *The Raw Garden* was made a Poetry Book Society Choice, and *Short Days, Long Nights* a Poetry Book Society Recommendation. In 1989 she won second prize in the *Times Literary Supplement*/Cheltenham Literature Festival Poetry Competition, and in 1990 first prize in the Cardiff International Poetry Competition. Her poems, short stories, poems for children and songs have appeared in a wide range of magazines and anthologies.

For the past ten years she has given public readings of her work at a variety of venues and for many different organisations all over Britain, including literature festivals, libraries, arts centres, Arvon Foundation centres, schools and universities, poetry groups and prisons. In 1989 she took part in the British Council-sponsored *Gedichte mit Schärfe* tour by Bloodaxe poets to Berlin, which involved poetry and jazz events, readings at the Free University and to high schools and residential course groups.

She took part in London's South Bank *Child of Europe* series of East European poetry readings in 1988, and in a series of Russian poetry events at the South Bank in April 1991. She has read her poetry for poetry programmes on Radio 3 and Radio 4, and has read and discussed her work on *Woman's Hour*. Her poetry has been filmed for BBC Television's *ArtsWest*. During autumn 1990 she held a poetry residency in Avon primary schools. In October 1990 she became Writer-in-Residence at the Polytechnic of Wales, and in May 1991 she was Writer-in-Residence at the Brighton Festival.

HELEN DUNMORE

SHORT DAYS LONG NIGHTS

NEW & SELECTED POEMS

BLOODAXE BOOKS

ISBN: 1 85224 150 0

First published 1991 by
Bloodaxe Books Ltd,
P.O. Box 1SN,
Newcastle upon Tyne NE99 1SN.

Bloodaxe Books Ltd acknowledges
the financial assistance of Northern Arts.

Typesetting by EMS Phototypesetting, Berwick upon Tweed,
and Bryan Williamson, Darwen, Lancashire.

Printed in Great Britain by
Bell & Bain Limited, Glasgow, Scotland.

For my family

Acknowledgements

This book includes poems selected from Helen Dunmore's previous collections, *The Apple Fall* (1983), *The Sea Skater* (1986) and *The Raw Garden* (1988), all published by Bloodaxe Books.

For the poems in the first section, acknowledgements are due to the editors of the following publications in which some of those poems first appeared: *Argo, Giant Steps, High on the Walls* (Morden Tower/Bloodaxe Books, 1990), *The Honest Ulsterman, London Magazine, New Statesman, The Observer, The Orange Dove of Fiji* (Hutchinson, 1989), *Oxford Magazine, Poetry Book Society Anthology 1988-1989* and *1989-1990* (PBS/Hutchinson, 1988 & 1989), *Poetry London Newsletter, Poetry Review, The Rialto, Soho Square* (Bloomsbury, 1989), *Spectator, Times Literary Supplement*, and *Verse.*

'Sisters leaving before the dance' won first prize in the City of Cardiff International Poetry Competition in 1990, and 'The dream-life of priests' won 2nd prize in the *Times Literary Supplement*/Cheltenham Literature Fesitval Poetry Competition in 1989.

The cover photograph is reproduced by kind permission of Sidney Moulds/Science Photo Library. It shows a polarised light micrograph of crystals of a Migraleve tablet, a treatment for migraine, containing paracetamol, codeine phosphate, buclizine hydrochloride and dioctyl sodium sulphosuccinate.

Contents

SHORT DAYS, LONG NIGHTS (1991)

THE APPLE FALL (1983)

THE SEA SKATER (1986)

THE RAW GARDEN (1988)

SHORT DAYS, LONG NIGHTS

NEW POEMS

Those shady girls

Those shady girls on the green side of the street,
those far-from-green girls who keep to the shade,
those shady girls in mysterious suits
with their labels half-showing
as the cream flap of the jacket swings open,
those girls kicking aside the front-panelled pleats
of their cream suits with cerise lapels,

those on-coming girls,
those girls swinging pearly umbrellas
as tightly-sheathed as tulips in bud
from an unscrupulous street-seller,
those girls in cream and cerise suits
which mark if you touch them,
those girls with their one-name appointments
who walk out of the sunshine.

The dream-life of priests

Do they wake careless and warm
with light on the unwashed windows
and a perpetual smell of bacon,

do their hearts sink at today's martyr
with his unpronounceable name
and strange manner of execution?

Do they wake out of the darkness
with hearts thudding like ours
and reach for the souvenir lamp-switch

then shove a chair against the door
and key facts into the desk-top computer
while cold rattles along the corridor?

Do they cry out in sleep
at some barely-crushed thought,
some failure to see the joke,

or do they rest in their dreams
along the surface of the water
like a bevy of dragonflies

slack and blue in the shallows
whirring among reed-mace and water-forget-me-not
while the ripples cluck?

Do they wake in ordinary time
to green curtains slapping the frame
of a day that'll cloud later on,

to cars nudging and growling for space,
to a baptismal mother, wan with her eagerness
and her sleepless, milk-sodden nights?

Do they reach and stroke the uneven plaster
and sniff the lime-blossom threading
like silk through the room,

or do they wait, stretched out like babies
in the gold of its being too early
with sun on their ceilings wobbling like jelly

while their housekeepers jingle the milk-bottles
and cry 'Father!' in sixty-year-old voices
and scorch toast with devotion –

do they sense the milk in the pan rising
then dive with their blue chins, blundering
through prayer under their honeycomb blankets?

Sisters leaving before the dance

Sisters leaving before the dance,
before the caller gets drunk
or the yellow streamers unreel
looping like ribbons
here and there on the hair of the dancers,

sisters at the turn of the stairs
as the sound system
one-twos, as the squeezebox
mewed in its case

is slapped into breath, and that scrape
of the tables shoved back for the dance
burns like the strike of a match
in the cup of two hands.
Ripe melons and meat

mix in the binbags with cake
puddled in cherry-slime, wind
heavy with tar
blows back the yard door, and I'm

caught with three drinks in my hands
on the stairs looking up
at the sisters leaving before the dance,
not wishing to push past them
in their white broderie anglaise and hemmed

skirts civilly drawn
to their sides to make room
for the big men in suits,
and the girls in cerise

dance-slippers and cross-backed dresses
who lead the way up
and take charge of the tickets, and yet
from their lips canteloupe
fans as they speak

in bright quick murmurs between
a violin ghosting a tune
and the kids in the bar downstairs
begging for Coke, peaky but certain.

The sisters say their *good nights*
and all the while people stay bunched
on the stairs going up, showing respect
for the small words of the ones leaving,
the ones who don't stay for the dancing.

One sister twists a white candle
waxed in a nest of hydrangeas –
brick-red and uncommon, flowers
she really can't want – she bruises the limp

warm petals with crisp fingers
and then poises her sandal
over the next non-slip stair
so the dance streams at her heels
in the light of a half-shut door.

On not writing certain poems

You put your hand over mine and whispered
'There he is, laying against the pebbles' –
you wouldn't point for the shadow
stirring the trout off his bed
where he sculled the down-running water,

and the fish lay there, unbruised
by the soft knuckling of the river-bed
or your stare which had found him out.

Last night I seemed to be walking
with something in my hand, earthward, down-
dropping as lead, unburnished –

a plate perhaps or a salver
with nothing on it or offered
but its own shineless composure.

I have it here on my palm, the weight
settled, spreading through bone
until my wrist tips backward, pulled down

as if my arm was laid in a current
of eel-dark water – that thrum
binding the fingers – arrow-like –

Our clear hands

Our clear hands
mix fingers
we're ringless
on purpose
or are we
were you always
after something else
were you always
feeling less close

when we held hands
and there was no
friction of gold

we're ringless
on purpose
we chose
or did we
were you always

Privacy of rain

Rain. A plump splash
on tense, bare skin.
Rain. All the May leaves
run upward, shaking.

Rain. A first touch
at the nape of the neck.
Sharp drops kick the dust, white
downpours shudder
like curtains, rinsing
tight hairdos to innocence.

I love the privacy of rain,
the way it makes things happen
on verandahs, under canopies
or in the shelter of trees
as a door slams and a girl runs out
into the black-wet leaves.
By the brick wall an iris
sucks up the rain
like intricate food, its tongue
sherbetty, furred.

Rain. All the May leaves
run upward, shaking.
On the street bud-silt
covers the windscreens.

Dancing man

That lake lies along the shore
like a finger down my cheek,

its waters lull and collapse
dark as pomegranates,

the baby crawls on the straw
in the shadow-map of his father's chair

while the priest talks things over
and light dodges across his hair.

There's a lamp lit in the shed
and a fire on, and a man drinking

spiritus fortis he's made for himself.
But on the floor of the barn

the dancing man is beginning to dance.
First a beat from the arch of his foot

as he stands upright, a neat
understatement of all that's in him

and he lowers his eyes to her
as if it's nothing, nothing –

but she has always wanted him.
Her baby crawls out from the chairs

and rolls in his striped vest laughing
under the feet of the dancers

so she must dance over him
toe to his cheek, heel to his hair,

as she melts to the man dancing.
They are talking and talking over there –

the priest sits with his back to her
for there's no malice in him

and her husband glistens like the sun
through the cypress-flame of the man dancing.

In the shed a blackbird
has left three eggs which might be kumquats –

they are so warm. One of them's stirring –
who said she had deserted them?

In the orchard by the barn
there are three girls wading,

glossy, laughing at something,
they spin a bucket between them,

glowing, they are forgotten –
something else is about to happen.

At Cabourg II

The bathers, where are they? The sea is quite empty,
lapsed from its task of rinsing the white beach.

The promenade has a skein of walkers, four to the mile,
like beads threaded on the long Boulevard in front of the flowers.

Shutters are all back on the bankers' fantasy houses,
but the air inside is glassy as swimming-pool water,

no one breathes there or silts it with movement.
Out of the kitchen a take-away steam rises:

the bankers are having sushi in honour of their guests
who are here, briefly, to buy 'an impressionist picture'.

A boy is buried up to his neck in sand
but the youth leader stops another who pretends to piss on him.

The rest draw round, they have got something helpless:
his head laid back on its platter of curls.

With six digging, he's out in a minute.
They oil his body with Ambre Solaire,

two boys lay him across their laps, a third
wipes at his feet then smiles up enchantingly.

Baron Hardup

I see the boys at the breakwater
straighten now, signalling friends,
and the little imperious one who is just not
dinted at the back of the arms
with child-like softness
sticks up his thumb to mark the next leap.

This far off it's peaceful to watch them
while I'm walking ahead barefoot
on a wide, grey Norman promenade,
thinking of the Baron de Charlus
not in his wheelchair but younger,
bumbling into seduction in a hot courtyard,

tipped upside-down like a sand-timer,
labelled implacably – 'the invert'
caught at the wide-striped
dawn years of the century
where the candy of skirts blows inward and outward
to a pure, bellying offshore wind.

The beautiful line of his coat ripples –
he's Baron Hardup with dreams tupping
like pantomime horses – he fixes his eyeglass
and glares at the waves with passionate indecisiveness
as if to stop, or not stop, their irregular fall,
while the boys figure what he is good for.

Albertine in the underworld

In her dreams she was off elsewhere,
blinking, luxuriant, deep
in the feathers of her lover's
escaping back-hair.

You were right, of course, to suspect her.
Your constant sleeper had slipped off
leaving her bare self on the bed's hollow,

and though your hands held the clue
you lay there, letting her flesh
fill the imprint that said *beautiful.*

Scuffing the path with her heels she flew,
preoccupied, a little self-righteous –
the thrice-welcome visitor

who knows that in fairness
even as you grasp her
she has to smile over your shoulder.

At Doncières

Past twelve with night dropping in handfuls –
even laughter can't move through it.

Softly impulsive breezes like tongue-licks
flicker the shutter-bars,

the bowl of a wine-glass responds and sings
to a finger easing apart its music

while its cross-plaited stem of glass wire shimmers
as if aching – the same touch teases it.

Dark spurs of wine lie on the cloth
after the toasts. A newly-sprung sweat-dew

breaks on the twenty-year-old lieutenant's forehead.
He sits there, glittering, wine-blank,

until his neighbour eases a napkin
out of the table-long wreck of crushed linen

and prints off the still face of his friend
whose eyes beneath the cloth don't shift.

Nearly May Day

After a night jagged by guard-dogs and nightingales
I sit to be videoed
at the corner of this carved balcony
where ten o'clock sun falls
past the curve of the Berlin Wall.
It's nearly May Day.
Just here there's a double wall –
a skin of concrete, a skin of stone
the colour of the Alsatians.

My feet shift on the slats.
I want to comb my hair straight.
I have my back
to a wood in the closed zone –
an orchard's bright pelt
sparkling with blossom tips.
Bees fly in purposeful zigzags
over the Wall, tracing their map
of air and nectar.
Each day they fly through the spoors
of air-wiping floodlights now
sheathed in the watch-towers
to this one apple tree
which makes a garden of itself
under the balcony.

I have my back to the church.
Its roof glows in the gaps
where slate after slate's peeled off.
I have my back to the porch
with its red lining of valerian,
its sound like a cough
as the doors squeeze themselves shut.
Katja unrolls cable
over the balcony rail.
A double wiring of roses
straddles the pews
in a hamlet which is the other half of here,
clear and suggestive as a mirror.

They say nobody lives there
but guards' wives and children.
You rarely see them,
they melt into the woods like foxes
but you hear their motorbikes miles off
clutching the road surface.
You might hear the guards' wives say
'Let the kids have the grapes'
just as the nightingales insist
for hours when you can't sleep.

This hamlet's like something I've dreamed
in a dream broken by rain,
with its lilac and dull green
tenderly shifting leaves,
its woodpiles,
its watched inhabitants,
wives of the guards
who have between them a little son
in a too-tight yellow jersey
flashing along their own balcony.

He runs from his steep-roofed home
to scrabble onto his tricycle
and race with fat frantic legs pedalling
the few square metres marked by the wives
with a shield-square of clothes-line
where they're forever hanging things out
while my back's turned.
I study the guards' underpants
and wish I still smoked
so I could blow smoke-rings
from the balcony of Jagdschloss Glienicke
past the flowering jaws of the apple tree
over complicated roof-shells
to the child himself.
I'd wave, holding the cigarette
cupped behind my back.

Any time they choose
people are changing Deutschmarks
for a tick on cheap paper,
a day-trip to the East
to buy Bulgarian church music
and butter at half-price,
to check their faces in a mirror
and get it all on video.
to walk through a map of mirrors
into the other half of here.

There's mist on the Glienicke bridge.
The flags are limp.
There's nothing flying at all –
not a flag, not an aeroplane
racing down safe corridors.

It's nearly May Day.
A riot's ripening in Kreuzberg.
If this is Spring, it's going on elsewhere
grasping horse-chestnut buds
in sticky hands
warm and forgetful
as a child who buries himself
for joy in Pankow's warm sands.

[September 1989]

Three workmen with blue pails

Three workmen with blue pails
swerve past an election poster
wrapped round a lamp-post pillar,

signed with a single carnation
and a name for each ward.
The workmen guffaw –

it's five past three on a small street
which traipses off Unter den Linden
deep into East Berlin.

Short, compact and bored
they tramp over the slats
where the pavement's torn up.

One of them's telling a joke.
They swing on under a banner
for a play by Harold Pinter –

stretched linen, four metres wide
and at least two workmen tall,
spread on a ten-metre wall –

the play's *The Dumb Waiter.*
They go on past a kindergarten
which is tipping out children,

past banks with bullet-holes in them,
past an industrial shoal
of tower-block homes

to the second-right turn
where the pulse of street-life picks up,
where there are people and shops.

Ahead, a queue forms
as a café rattles itself open
and starts to serve out ice cream.

Inside his treacle-brown frame
a young man flickers and smiles
as he fans out the biscuit-shells –

already half the ice cream's gone
and the waiter teases the children
with cold smoke from a new can.

Seeds stick to their tongues –
gooseberry, cloudberry – chill,
grainy and natural.

Shoving their caps back
the workmen join on
and move forward in line

for what's over. Tapping light coins
they move at a diagonal
to a blue, skew-whiff ditched Trabbi.

Brown coal

The room creaked like a pair of lungs
and the fire wouldn't go
till we held up the front page for it.
All the while the news was on

that day they wired up the Wall
while I was swimming on newspaper –
a cold rustle of words
to the wheezing of my sister.

I caught the fringe of her scarf
in winter smogs after school
as she towed me through the stutter
of high-lamped Ford Populars

and down the mouth of the railway tunnel
into water-pocked walls
and the dense sulphurous hollows
of nowhere in particular.

It was empty but for smog.
Coughing through our handkerchiefs
we walked eerily, lammed
at the brickwork, picked ourselves up.

I walked through nowhere last April
into a mist of brown coal,
sulphur emissions, diesel
stopped dead at the Wall,

the whiff of dun Trabants
puttering north/south
past a maze of roadworks,
leaving hours for us to cross

in the slow luxury of strolling
as the streets knit themselves up
to become a city again.
By instinct I kept my mouth shut

and breathed like one of us girls
in our "identical-twin" coats,
listening out for rare cars,
coal at the back of our throats –

it was England in the fifties,
half-blind with keeping us warm,
so I was completely at ease
in a small street off Unter Den Linden

as a fire-door behind wheezed
and Berlin creaked like two lungs.

Safe period

Your dry voice from the centre of the bed
asks 'Is it safe?'

and I answer for the days as if I owned them.
Practised at counting, I rock
the two halves of the month like a cradle.

The days slip over their stile
and expect nothing. They are just days,

and we're at it again, thwarting
souls from the bodies they crave.

They'd love to get into this room
under the yellow counterpane
we've torn to make a child's cuddly,

they'd love to slide into the sheets
between soft, much-washed
flannelette fleece,

they'd love to be here in the moulded spaces
between us, where there is no room,

but we don't let them. They fly about gustily,
noisy as our own children.

Big barbershop man

Big barbershop man turning away,
sides of his face
lathered and shaved
close with the cut-throat
he always uses,

big barbershop man turning away,
helping the neighbours
make good, sweating
inside a stretched t-shirt
with NO MEANS YES on the back of it,

waltzing a side of pig,
taking the weight,
scalp like a glove
rucked with the strain,
big barbershop man turning away
trim inside like a slice of ham

big barbershop man
hoisting the forequarter,
fat marbled with meat
stiff as a wardrobe,

big barbershop man
waltzing a side of pig
striped like a piece
of sun awning, cool
as a jelly roll,
big barbershop man waltzing the meat
like a barber's pole on yellow Main Street.

The Easter tree

To make an Easter tree last April
I tied three or four puffs of mimosa
with yellow ribbon and hooked them
over the whitewashed forks of a birch-branch
so they'd bounce there like canaries
in a side-draught from the window.
– God, when I think of that flight
through the invisibility of my own life
I've made often, at two a.m.
when there's a wind and the curtain ticks
on its pole like a bird's claw
turning its fluff-ball over and over –

It was warm, and for three days
the mimosa made a disturbance
as it shook out its perfume
into the dusty folds of the room.
We played KING SUNNY ADE
at all hours between ceremonies,
I thought of the first wind from the orange groves
as you drive down to Valencia
towards the white-hooded wizards of Easter.

A woman in a yellow bikini
sat on the pebbles near Brighton pier
with a man 'old enough to be her father':
one of the club that swims through the winter
and spent Holy Week by a breakwater
flopping, docile as seals
from belly to backside, thighs creased
from four decades of daily commuting.
She was either grey or ash-blonde,
with her wide back smoothly tanned
or else the lizard-brown of the beach habituée.
She stayed there with her back to us
straining the brief yellow of her bikini.
Later I saw them promenading,
solicitous, heads down.

This was on the Easter Monday
with a spill of cars on the tarmac,
skewed as if their inhabitants had run
on seeing water and sun.

For three days I didn't need much sleep.
My dreams stayed filmic and tight
screening what I wanted to remember:
a buffet table in front of me
where a neat half-bottle of wine shimmered
and I shut my eyes as the TGV
swerved on its well of suspension
towards the next stop at Orange.
When I woke they were still shouting its name
like the secret end of a declension
while the engine itched, idled,
and groomed itself in a smell of asbestos.

Then I stood under the plane trees,
wedged and swayed by the weight
of older, more knowledgeable bodies,
arms pressed to my sides, face sun-sore.
We were a barrel of anchovies, upright and glinting
with silver hair-combs and sun-dazzled faces
slewed leftward for the procession
when a hail of sharp-sided bonbons
stung on our right cheeks
and the crowd broke, shielding itself.
A woman with a cone of grey paper
helped me to gather
the yellow sweets I did not want.
She held out her cone like the market woman
where I bought my allowance of loquats,
then there was a stir of genuflections
like the lying-low of small mammals
when a hawk's shadow crosses the fields.

By Low Week distemper had flaked
from the damp skin of the birch,
and the airy cost of the mimosa

still had to be paid
though its flower-balls shrank up like birds' claws
scratching as they try to recapture
the boneless stun of their first flight.

They say that for the plane tree
to peel off its yearly pollution
is easy as winking.
I lean my face into its bark
now that the crowds have gone,
press my cheek against two clumsily-cut hearts
and turn the sweets in my pocket
over and over, for luck.

The dry well

It was not always a dry well.
Once it had been brimming with water,
cool, limpid, delicious water,
but a man came and took water from the well
and a woman came and took water from the well
and a man took water from the well again

and the well could not drink
from the low, slack water-table.

The well lacked a sense of its own danger
and a man came to take water from the well
and a woman came to take water from the well

but as the man was coming again
the well sighed in the dry darkness,
the well spoke in a quiet voice
from the deep-down bell of its emptiness
Give me some water.

But the man was at work with his heavy bucket
and he cried cheerfully, *Wait half a minute,*
I will just draw one more bucketful!

When he swung it up it was full of dust
and he was angry with the well.
Could it not have held out longer?
He had only needed one more bucketful.

Our family, swimming again

Our family, swimming again.
Slick lily-ropes, flat as gelled hair,
pull under the surface.
The four lads with an army feel to them
grin and are gone
leaving the splash of their voices
like a high-water-mark, drying
on the concrete landing-stage
where we splay and bake in the sun.

My husband says he's standing on sand
and can touch its clean ribs with his feet,
but I hang, vertical,
sleeved with the cold, my mouth level
with the smooth purl of the current
like yards of candy being pulled,
while in a hospital core
sticky as the inside of wedding-cake,
snail-vaulted ear-walls
fill up with electricity.

This current's for hauling us off
by the hair, making it flow upright.
Yes, but I might
yet side-slip or trick it.
For all the cover my clothes give
I may as well swim naked.

A physiotherapist sighs with the heat
as she bends, unplaiting the tendons
healed wrong in my father's feet.
He hears her dap off down the corridor
then feels in his right-hand drawer
and works away with the polish I gave him
to make a mid-tan gloss on his sandals.
There's a quick, willowy landscape in yellows
done by the Sinhalese charge-nurse –

but this is not a poem about him.
I like the look of what it's not.
For a moment out of reach
in my bra with its lace half-off
I'm just swimming unexpectedly
under the vaults of the aqueduct,
kicking free of the lilies
which thrust bare buds inches above me.

My husband calls me to stop.
I tip on my back and stare up
the vaults' inner greased walls.
There's a man watching me swim,
one big hand clamped to the parapet,
the other combing for sounds on his Walkman.

Sweet pepper

See, you have fallen asleep in spite of me
and my heels going and returning,
with your blankets rucked and your hard-eyed toy dog
wedged under your arm.

In your dream two children are climbing a summer mountain.
They pass the snake-pit, tangled and blue
with smoke of sliding yellow and black snakes –

these will not hurt you. Your brother and Becky
branch like skaters from path fork to path
and so upwards and gone, with the thin girl

driving ahead, and the slower
graceful, compact boy stopped, lingering
over a stand of flowerless balsam.

See, you throw out your hand to the wall
where the children are crying and laughing
after their day lost on the mountain –
but here the sky sweats with excess of rain,

you're far away from yourself, and I'm
unjamming the window to night air
soaked through with the storm, bruised
fresh as a sweet pepper.

Heron

It's evening on the river,
steady, milk-warm,

the nettles head-down
with feasting caterpillars,

the current turning,
thin as a blade-bone.

Reed-mace shivers.
I'm miles from anywhere.

Who's looking?
did a fish jump?

– and then a heron goes up
from its place by the willow.

With ballooning flight
it picks up the sky

and makes off, loaded.
I wasn't looking,

I heard the noise of its wings
and I turned,

I thought of a friend,
a cool one with binoculars,

here's rarity
with big wing-flaps, suiting itself.

One yellow chicken

One yellow chicken
she picks up expertly and not untenderly
from the conveyor of chickens.

Its soft beak gobbles feverishly
at a clear liquid which might be
a dose of sugar-drenched serum –

the beak's flexible membrane
seems to engulf the chicken
as it tries to fix on the dropper's glass tip.

Clear yellow juice gulps through a tube
and a few drops, suddenly colourless,
swill round a gape wide as the brim of a glass

but the chicken doesn't seem afraid –
or only this much, only for this long
until the lab assistant flicks it back on
to the slowly moving conveyor of chickens
and it tumbles, catches itself,
then buoyed up by the rest
reels out of sight, cheeping.

On Richard's farm

We climb, guided by yellowing smoke signals
and a brief scribble of figures, seen
then gone as smoke whirls between us.
Where the hillside was waist-high in brambles
we slip on mud and tangles of root.
The ground's flaky with ash-puddles
from yesterday's burning. There are orange-mackintoshed
armloads of saplings, kids from the Youth Club
dragging up bracken with rakes, a second clearing-gang
close to the skyline
and a plantation stuck in among all this
as if in spite of it.

Wet dogwoods poke from their plastic sacks.
I bend to finger the sharp
points of the buds. No one knows much
but we pick out the easy ones: black-budded ash,
oak with its last year's leaves,
and where the stems are labelled, we read
field maple, wayfaring tree, dog-rose,
guelder and small-leaved lime, willow and hawthorn.

The boys edge off, making away down two fields
until they're free of us, crouched,
wrestling the door of a broken-down horsebox.
One at each side, like nurses,
we make the measured-up beds quickly,
angling the beeches into a spade-slit
in the soil's uncomfortable smoothness.
One wedges, the other stamps down.
There's no back-garden stir
of peat and bonemeal around their root-hairs.
The earth's like a frog's lips on them: dense, cool.

The boys lag along the ditch-bank
and stop to cup their hands in the water.
They lean out, peering for fish.
One steps on the pondweed and sinks thighdeep.

His arms whirr as the other one hauls
till the boot sucks free, and he hops barefoot
drying himself, then both suddenly bundle
into a gap under the hedge.

Near Berwick last August
I was waiting out at a gate for them
and looking for the next train
up the Edinburgh main line
which drove through the farmland.
It was late when they came up the field-path,
heads close, examining
a dead shrew they'd found in the stubble.
The train necklaced behind them
between the farm and the Holy Island
and then it coiled and sprang north
with long hoots to the bare fields.

Those three parallel fields across the valley
from Richard's farm: one of them's hired grazing,
blond, sheep-cropped; one of them's his.
He points to its noticeable greenness,
a depth you'd feel if you went close.
Behind, there's the bang of stakes going in
where the wood's being built,
and a flash of sun from the pale-yellow
rabbit-proof tree-guards.
In fifteen years he'll take out the larch,
leaving the oak and beech unperturbed.

We've planted thirty beech trees together.
We stop, and yell to the boys.
There are fresh shadows on the cleared hillside
as our spade makes an intersection
between the trees' height and the length of our lives.
We feel the sun as we wait for them,
and here we are in an old photograph
taken one hot Sunday on Richard's farm
in the summer of '79. I'm ducking aside
into the shelter of my hair,
my skin prickling with sunburn, its cells
on edge to the awkwardness

encoded in this July pastoral,
and I let drop the hand I'm holding.
– But in fact I didn't notice the camera.
The image came later, a pure souvenir
from the division of the photograph albums.

Behind us, in the over-exposed background,
Ollie clambers the warm furrows,
his shoulders burning along the strap-marks
of his American Depression workwear.
He wanted to pick off the courgette flowers –
I remember cajoling him
so he'd hold one yellow trumpet all afternoon.
Now the beeches fend for themselves
with black plastic spread round their stems.
Weeds coil under the mulch, blanching,
and the saplings' ribbon-smooth bark imperceptibly toughens
minute by minute, airbrushed from without
like the skin-grain of the child who's become
my dark-haired stepson.

Our car's alongside the barn, arrested
in a haze of January mildness.
The new calves stumble and look up
out of their straw, but we've nothing to give them.
They fold back, easy, at home,
while a single sheep that's penned in with them
niggles its way through a bale.

In this unseasonable slack end of Sunday
people come walking, some from the village,
some over the bridge, some sudden as if born
on the sun-warmed flanks of the farm.
One group trails over the fields
soberly, keeping the footpath.
A girl comes last, jarring her pushchair,
gives us an incurious glance
then bites her lip for the next lunge
over the dry ruts.

For a moment my heart tightens
at the baby's thistle-white hair,
then a drizzle of sound crosses the valley
like a rain-column straying miles off.
It's pouring elsewhere: we're glad,
and the girl shoves on, berating the child
with an irregular impatience
which is almost motherly.

Sailing to Cuba

I'd climbed the crab-apple in the wind
that wild season of Cuba,

I leaned out on the twigs
to where clouds heeled over like sails
on the house-bounded horizon,

but even from here I felt the radio throb
like someone who was there when the accident happened
'not two yards from where I was standing',

then Big Band music cha-cha'd from room to room
to fill in time between news.

At school we learned 'Quinquireme of Nineveh
from distant Ophir...' The ships nudged closer.
The wind roared to itself like applause.

Off the West Pier

Dropped yolks of shore-lamp quiver on tarmac –
the night's disturbed and the sea itself
sidles about after its storm, buttery,
melting along the groynes.

The sea's a martinet with itself,
will come this far and no farther
like a Prussian governess
corrupted by white sugar –

Oh but the stealth
with which it twitches aside mortar
and licks, and licks
moist grains off the shore.

By day it simply keeps marching
beat after beat like waves of soldiers
timed to the first push. In step with the music
it swells greenness and greyness, spills foam
onto a fly-swarming tide-line –
beertabs and dropped King Cones,
flotsam of inopportune partners
sticky with what came after.

A man lies on his back
settled along the swell, his knees
glimmering, catching a lick of moonlight,
lazy as a seagull on Christmas morning –
He should have greased himself with whale-blubber
like a twelve-year-old Goddess-chested
cross-Channel swimmer.
His sadness stripes through him like ink
leaving no space for him.
He paws slow arm sweeps and rolls
where the sea shoulders him.

Up there an aeroplane falters,
its red landing-lights on
scouting the coast home.
The pilot smokes a cigarette.
Its tip winks with each breath.

Winter 1955

We're strung out on the plain's upthrust,
bubbles against the sill of the horizon.
Already the dark folds each figure to itself
like a mother putting on her child's overcoat,
or a paid attendant, who quickly and deftly
slots goose-pimpled arms into their stoles.

My own mother is attending to her daughters
in the Christmas gloom of our long garden
before the others are born.
A stream's tongue takes its first courses:
in siren suits and our cheek-hugging bonnets
we put one foot each in that water.

Now standstill clumps sink and disappear
over the plate-edge of the world.
The trees hold up fingers like candelabra,
blue and unsure as the word 'distant'.
Casually heeled there, we circle
the New Look skirts of our mother.

The attendant's hands skim on a breast
fused into party-going ramparts of taffeta,
but he takes up his gaze into the hall
as if there's nothing to be sorry or glad for,
and nothing in the snowy eternity
that feathers his keyhole.

There was no music in Padua

'There was no music in Padua
when I was there

and could predict concertos
down from the slope of their openings

and charm birds from their branches –
how they sighed and resisted...'

But there his memory bars it –
the bird in the hand bobbing
with song left in it – the hand tensing –

the soul softened for once to its predators
who lounge the black-and-white corners of Padua.

He looks for peace and subtracts people,
but there on the bridge once, fishing,
he saw the twist of an arm
come up whitely – it was a girl folding
the plain sheet of her rain-soaked hair
into her collar –

Handing-on of dreams

I want to spare you the jolts of a "good" journey
through the lock system of another country,
where poplared canals bind the horizon without harming it
and pull you into their dreams. You would spend years
learning the language which now flies bird-like
out of your tongue's thicket.

Or let's say I'm inoculating you
with the nightly row of the typewriter
and piles of discontented paper by the table.
I make poetry common as floor-washing

but still you wade in, thigh-deep in dreams
at nine-thirty, while we are doped
on one sofa, numb to excellent acting.
On-screen, the occupation of France.
Trains shake the canal bridge.

We put you between us, cold
from dreams in your too-short karate pyjamas.
We could sleep here, in a triptych of flesh
while television patters in the corner like rainfall

or let's say it would be easier than going upstairs.
The music of the wheels hesitates
on the about-to-be-exploded bridge –
but we lay you back in the sheet-hung nest
you've made for yourself.

Rinsing

In the corded hollows of the wood
leaves fall.
How light it is.
The trees are rinsing themselves of leaves
like Degas laundresses, their forearms
cold with the jelly-smooth
blue of starch-water.

The laundresses lean back and yawn
with their arms still in the water
like beech-boughs, pliant
on leavings of air.

In the corded hollows of the wood
how light it is.
How my excitement
burns in the chamber.

To Betty, swimming

You're breast-up in the bubbling spaces you make for yourself,
your head in the air, pointy, demure,
ridiculous in its petalled swim-cap.

You chug slowly across the pool.
Your legs trail. Your arms won't sweep
more than a third of the full stroke,

yet when you look up you're curling with smiles,
complicit as if splashed
with mile-deep dives from the cliff's height.

In Berber's Ice Cream Parlour

A fat young man in BERBER'S ICE CREAM PARLOUR
under a tiled ceiling the colour of farm butter
with a mirror at 45° to his jaw.

His moist jowls, lucent and young
as the tuck where a baby's buttock and thigh join,
quiver a little, preparing
to meet the order he's given.

A tall glass skims the waitress's breasts.
He holds on, spoon poised
to see if the syrup'll trickle right

past the mound of chopped nuts to the ice-
white luscious vanilla sheltering
under its blanket of cream.

The yellow skin weakens and melts.
He devotes himself,
purses his lips to wrinkling-point,

digs down with the long spoon
past jelly and fruit
to the depths, with the cool
inching of an expert.

Beside him there's a landscape in drained pink
and blue suggesting the sea
with an audacious cartoon economy.
They've even put in one white triangle
to make the horizon. A sail.

Large creamy girls mark the banana splits
with curls and squiggles,
pour sauce on peach melbas,
thumb in real strawberries.

Their bodies sail behind the counters,
balloons tight at the ropes, held down
by a customer's need for more clotted cream
topping on his three-tier chocolate sundae.

They have eight tables to serve.
With their left hands they slap out the change
and cornets smelling of nickel
for kids' take-away treats,

and over on the bar counter there's room
for adult, luxurious absorption
of dark mocha ice cream.

Flowing, damp-curled, the waitresses
pass with their trays
doubled by mirrors, bumping like clouds.

On drinking lime juice in September

(for Patrick Charnley)

How the sick body calms itself
and knows it is blissful to live.
The lime juice of long voyages
fans through each tissue.

Ultramarine stands at the masts,
the long wake purls, barbarous sailors
wait round the canvas, heads bowed.

The captain, your ancestor,
fell from the grace of his life one voyage
west from Australia. They made him
his shroud of sailcloth with quick stitches.

They stole his book of the burial service
out of his pocket: now it was theirs
to read through slowly, becalmed
in its long, sea-remembering cadences.

They launched his vessel of flesh
where it would dive, darken,
cast up its sewn air,
its gene code with a hundred answers.

Deep in the story

Their sides buff through the fog –
Friesians got loose
up to the window, making the room dark.
Their breath spreads on the glass
as I dress quickly, my back to your smile.

I stoop to feel for my tights
but you don't stir. You lie padded, reliving
a walk last year in country you liked
when you fanned arms to frighten the cattle
bunched at our next stile.
They froze as you came too close.

I remember the train home.
You had your city-going coat on again,
your collar sharp as an owl's wings
as it glides under beeches, white-faced,
supping its night rounds.

You got me to come under your coat
though it wasn't that cold.
Collusive, quick-breathing,
we made the most of a snow-spatter,
holed up in a weather bleep, a pretence of danger
as the signal stayed down for an hour
and a fan of dirty heat cooled at our ankles.

Slow jaws crunched at the frost.
The guard waded through midnight
mouth wide, lowing
words I couldn't catch.
At our window he swung up his lantern
then you were bluffing each other
two men knowing the score.

The lantern rocked and moved on
while the snow chivvied, and we
looked at each other, deep
in the story you'd later be telling.

Not going to the forest

If you had said the words 'to the forest'
at once I would have gone there
leaving my garden of broccoli and potato-plants.

I would not have struggled

to see the last ribbons of daylight
and windy sky tear over the crowns
of the oaks which stand here,
heavy draught animals
bearing, continually bearing.

I would have rubbed the velvety forest
against my cheek like the pincushion
I sewed with invisible stitches.

No. But you said nothing
and I have a child to think of
and a garden of parsnips and raspberries.
It's not that I'm afraid,
but that I'm still gathering
the echoes of my five senses –

how far they've come with me, how far
they want to go on.

So the whale-back of the forest
shows for an instant, then dives.
I think it has oxygen within it
to live, downward, for miles.

Lutherans

Whichever way I turned on the radio
there was Sibelius
or an exceptionally long weather forecast.
Good practice: I'd purse up my lips
to the brief gulp of each phrase.

Sometimes I struck a chord with the World Service's
sense-fuzz, like the smell of gardenia
perfume in Woolworth's: instantly cloying,
the kind that doesn't bloom on your skin,

or, in the two p.m. gloom of the town square,
I'd catch the pale flap of a poster
for the Helsingin Sanomat: POMPIDOU KUOLLUT.
I'd buy one, but never wrestle beyond the headline.

When pupils asked what I thought of 'this three-day week'
I'd mention the candle-blaze
nightly in my room during the power-cuts,
and the bronchitis I had,
but I'd balance the fact that I smoked too much
against the marsh-chill when the heating went off.

I'd always stop on the railway bridge
even at one in the morning. The city was shapeless, squeezed in
by hills bristling with Sitka spruce.
The drunks had their fires lit
but they were slow, vulnerable, frozen
while flaming on a half-litre from the State Alcohol Shop.

If their luck held they'd bunch on the Sports Hall heating-grates
rather than be chipped free from a snow heap
in the first light of ten in the morning,
among a confusion of fur-hatted burghers
going to have coffee and cakes.
Work started at eight, there was never enough time.
They'd stop, chagrined, and murmur 'It's shocking'.

They were slowly learning not to buy the full-cream milk
of their farming childhoods; there was a government campaign
with leaflets on heart disease and exercise
and a broadsheet on the energy crisis
with diagrams suggesting the angles
beyond which windows should never be opened.

Their young might be trim, but they kept
a pious weakness for sinning on cake
and for those cloudy, strokeable hats
that frame Lutheran pallor.
After an evening visit to gym, they'd roll
the green cocoon of their ski-suited baby
onto the pupils' table. Steadied with one hand
it lay prone and was never unpacked.

FROM THE APPLE FALL

(1983)

The marshalling yard

In the goods yard the tracks are unmarked.
Snow lies, the sky is full of it.
Its hush swells in the dark.

Grasped by black ice on black
a massive noise of breathing
fills the tracks;

cold women, ready for departure
smooth their worn skirts
and ice steals through their hands like children
from whose touch they have already been parted.

Now like a summer
the train comes
beating the platform
with its blue wings.

The women stir. They sigh.
Feet slide
warm on a wooden stairway
then a voice calls and
milk drenched with aniseed
drawls on the walk to school.

At last they leave.
Their breathless neighbours
steal from the woods, the barns,
and tender straw
sticks to their palms.

A cow here in the June meadow

A cow here in the June meadow
where clouds pile, tower above tower.

We lie, buried in sunburn,
our picnic a warm
paper of street tastes,

she like a gold cloud
steps, moony.
Her silky rump dips
into the grasses, buffeting
a mass of seed ready to run off in flower.

We stroll under the elder, smell
wine, trace blackfly along its leaf-veins

then burning and yawning we pile
kisses onto the hot upholstery.

Now evening shivers along the water surface.
The cow, suddenly planted, stands – her tender
skin pollened all over –
ready to nudge all night at the cold grasses,
her udder heavily and more heavily swinging.

Annunciation off East Street

The window swings and squeaks in the sun.
Mary says to the angel: 'Come.
My husband is sleepy.
You're rapid and warm-winged.'

First Elizabeth, breathless,
ties up her dates in her heart.
How can a woman be so fortunate?
'Precious baby,' they write on her chart.

Elizabeth the ageing primipara
reminded of her ancestress Sarah
who also slept with an old man.
Bearded, whuffling,
his flesh drew like chicken-skin.

Mary sat with Elizabeth
chopping up parsley, their breath
pregnant, settling the room.
Here Elizabeth crouched for six months
uterus bubbling
while Zacharias snipped the altar flame.

'So it turns out at last.
You and the holy spirit –
I guessed it.
We're both gigantic
at night, feeding our great babies.

I gorge where no one can see me,
count days, walk tiptoe
still fearing the bloody trickle.'

Mary answered her laughing:
'Elizabeth, let's tell them everything!'

Zelda

At Great Neck one Easter
were Scott
Ring Lardner
and Zelda, who sat
neck high in catalogues like reading cards

her hair in curl for
wild stories, applauded.
A drink, two drinks and a kiss.

Scott and Ring both love her –
gold-headed, sky-high Miss
Alabama. (The lioness
with still eyes and no affectations
doesn't come into this.)

Some visitors said she ought
to do more housework, get herself taught
to cook.
Above all, find some silent occupation
rather than mess up Scott's vocation.

In France her barriers were simplified.
Her husband developed a work ethic:
film actresses; puritan elegance;

tipped eyes spilling material
like fresh Americas. You see
said Scott   they know about work, like me.

You can't beat a writer for justifying adultery.

Zelda
always wanted to be a dancer

she said, writhing
among the gentians that smelled of medicine.

A dancer in a sweat lather is not beautiful.
A dancer's mind can get fixed.

Give me a wooden floor, a practice dress,
a sheet of mirrors and hours of labour

and lie me with my spine to the floor
supple   secure.

She handed these back too
with her gold head and her senses.

She asks for visits. She makes herself hollow
with tears, dropped in the same cup.
Here at the edge of her sensations
there is no chance.

Evening falls on her Montgomery verandah.
No cars come by. Her only visitor
his voice, slender along the telephone wire.

The Polish husband

The traffic halted
and for a moment
the broad green avenue
hung like a wave

while a woman crossing
stopped me and said

'Can you show me my wedding?
– In which church is it going to be held?'

The lorries hooted at her
as she stood there on the island
for her cloak fell back
and under it her legs were bare.
Her hair was dyed blonde
and her sad face deeply tanned.

I asked her 'What is the name of your husband?'
She wasn't sure, but she knew his first name was Joe,
she'd met him in Poland
and this was the time for the wedding.

There was a cathedral behind us
and a sign to the centre of the town.
'I am not an expert on weddings,'
I said, 'but take that honey-coloured building
which squats on its lawns like a cat –
at least there's music playing inside it.'

So she ran with her heels tapping
and the long, narrow folds of her cloak falling apart.
A veil on wire flew from her head,
her white figure ducked in the porch and blew out.

But Joe, the Polish man. In the rush of this town
I can't say whether she even found him
to go up the incense-heavy church beside him
under the bridal weight of her clothes,
or whether he was one of the lorry drivers
to whom her brown, hurrying legs were exposed.

The damson

Where have you gone
small child,
the damson bloom
on your eyes

the still heap
of your flesh
lightly composed
in a grey shawl,

your skull's pulse
stains you,
the veins slip deep.

Two lights burn
at the mouth of the cave
where the air's thin
and the tunnels boom
with your slippery blood.

Your unripe cheeks cling
to the leaves, to the wall,
but your grasp unpeels
and your bruises murmur

while blueness clouds
on the down of your eyes,
your tears erode
and your smile files

through your lips like a soldier
who shoots at the sky
and you flash up in silver;

where are you now
little one,
peeled almond,
damson bloom?

In Rodmell Garden

It's past nine and breakfast is over.
With morning frost on my hands I cross
the white grass, and go nowhere.

It's icy: domestic. A grain
of coffee burns my tongue. Its heat
folds into the first cigarette.

The garden and air are still.
I am a stone and the world falls from me.

I feel untouchable – a new planet
where life knows it isn't safe to begin.
From silver flakes of ash I shape
a fin and watch it with anguish.

I hear apples rolling above me;
November twigs; a bare existence –

my sister is a marvellous
dolphin, flanking her young.
Her blood flushes her skin

but mine is trapped. Occasional moments
allow me to bathe in their dumb sweetness.

My loose pips ripen. My night subsides
rushing, like the long glide of an owl.

Raw peace. A pale, frost-lit morning.
The black treads of my husband on the lawn
as he goes from the house to the loft
                                laying out apples.

The apple fall

In a back garden I'm painting
the outside toilet in shell and antelope.
The big domestic bramley tree
hangs close to me, rosy and leafless.
Sometimes an apple thumps
into the bushes I've spattered with turpentine
while my brush moves with a suck
over the burnt-off door frame.

Towels from the massage parlour
are out on the line next door:
all those bodies sweating into them
each day – the fabric stiffening –
towels bodiless and sex over.

I load the brush with paint again
and I hear myself breathing.
Sun slips off the wall
so the yard is cool
and lumbered with shadows,

and then a cannonade of apples
punches the wall and my arms,
the ripe stripes on their cheeks fall open,
flesh spurts and the juices fizz and glisten.

Pictures of a Chinese nursery

Yesterday my stepson came home with school photographs.
The image is altered:
no longer one child
rimmed with a photographer's background
smiling much as he does at home

but three or four placed at a table together
working at egg-boxes, tissue-paper
and friendship enough to shiver their absorbed faces.
'That's Jessica. Sometimes, she gives all of us a kiss.'
Others are pointed out for pissing in school flowerbeds.

On his wall I have stuck a poster of a Chinese nursery.
There is a river, a tree,
a wooden bridge, and far into the distance
thick-packed orchards fruiting and flowering.

On the verandah the children fall into place
as radiant parents stride to the field,

the nursery curls on itself
the day without clocks unfolds
and after dinner their songs fly onto the mountain
as far as the plum orchards where workers stop to eat rice.

Pharaoh's daughter

The slowly moving river in summer
where bulrushes, mallow and water forget-me-not
slip to their still faces.

A child's body
joins their reflections,

his plastic boat
drifts into midstream
and though I lean down to
brown water that smells of peppermint
I can't get at it:
my willow branch flails and pushes the boat outwards.

He smiles quickly
and tells me it doesn't matter;
my feet grip in the mud
and mash blue flowers under them.

Then we go home
masking with summer days the misery
that has haunted a whole summer.

I think once of the Egyptian woman
who drew a baby from the bulrushes
hearing it mew in the damp
odorous growth holding its cradle.

There's nothing here but the boat
caught by its string
and through this shimmering day I struggle
drawn down by the webbed
years, the child's life cradled within.

Domestic poem

So, how decisive a house is:
quilted, a net of blood and green
droops on repeated actions at nightfall.

A bath run through the wall
comforts the older boy sleeping
meshed in the odours of breath and Calpol

while in the maternity hospital
ancillaries rinse out the blood bottles;

the feel and the spore
of babies' sleep stays here.

Later, some flat-packed plastic
swells to a parachute of oxygen
holding the sick through their downspin,

now I am well enough, I
iron, and place the folded sheets in bags
from which I shall take them, identical,
after the birth of my child.

And now the house closes us,
                                    close on us,
like fruit we rest in its warm branches

and though it's time for the child to come
nobody knows it, the night passes

while I sleepwalk the summer heat.

Months shunt me and I bring you
like an old engine hauling the blue
spaces that flash between track and train time.

Mist rises, smelling of petrol's
burnt offerings, new born,

oily and huge, the lorries drum
on Stokes' Croft,

out of the bathroom mirror the sky
is blue and pale as a Chinese mountain.

and I breathe in.

It's time to go now. I take nothing
but breath, thinned.
A blown-out dandelion globe
might choose my laundered body to grow in.

Patrick I

Patrick, I cannot write
such poems for you as a father might
coming upon your smile,

your mouth, half sucking, half sleeping,
your tears shaken from your eyes like sparklers
break up the nightless weeks of your life:

lightheaded, I go to the kitchen
and cook breakfast, aching as you grow hungry.
Mornings are plain as the pages
of books in sedentary schooldays.

If I were eighty and lived next door
hanging my pale chemises on the porch
would I envy or pity my neighbour?

Polished and still as driftwood
she stands smoothing her dahlias;

liquid, leaking,
I cup the baby's head to my shoulder:

the child's a boy and will not share
one day these obstinate, exhausted mornings.

Patrick II

The other babies were more bitter than you
Patrick, with your rare, tentative cry,
your hours of sleep, snuffing the medical air.

Give me time for your contours, your fierce drinking.
Like land that has been parched for half a summer
and smiles, sticky with feeding

I have examined and examined you
at midnight, at two days; I have accompanied you
to the blue world on another floor of the hospital
where half-formed babies open their legs like anemones
and nurses, specialised as astronauts,
operate around the apnoea pillows.

But here you bloomed. You survived,
sticky with nectar. X-rayed, clarified,
you came back, dirty and peaceful.

And now like sunflowers settling their petals
for the last strokes of light in September
your eyes turn to me at 3 a.m.

You meet my stiff, mucousy face
and snort, beating your hand on my breast
as one more feed flows through the darkness, timed
to nothing now but the pull of your mouth.

Weaning

Cool as sleep, the crates ring.
Birds stir and my milk stings me;
you slip my grasp. I never find you
in dreams – only your mouth
not crying
your sleep still pressing on mine.

The carpets shush. The house back silences.
I turn with you, wide-lipped
blue figure

into the underground of babies
and damp mothers fumbling at bras

and the first callus grows on us
weaned from your night smiles.

Clinic day

The midwife whose omniscient hands
drew blood as I draw money out on Tuesdays
calls me to wait. We stand
half off the pavement, she spinning a bicycle pedal,
I rocking a pram.

She will be homeless she says by Friday.
But I can't help her. I want to respond to
her troubles with the sleeping flesh of the baby.
Useless. Her days of him are over.

Here at the clinic they know we are mothers.
I might avert all eyes from the baby,
tie a blue bead to his wrist,
not name him –

yet here they brazenly call him my son,
brandish his name on paper,
tell me how well he gets on.

Breathlessly evil fate stays
by their red door-posts on tiptoe:
they will not play.

Approaches to winter

Now I write off a winter of growth.
First, hands batting the air,
forehead still smeared,

– now, suddenly, he stands there
upright and rounded as a tulip.
The garden sparkles through the windows.

Dark and a heap in my arms;
the thermostat clicking all night.
Out in the road beached cars and winter
so cold five minutes would finish you.

Light fell in its pools
each evening. Tranquilly
it stamped the same circles.

Friends shifted their boots on the step.
Their faces gleamed from their scarves
that the withdrawal of day
brought safety.

Experience so stitched, intimate,
mutes me.
Now I'm desperate for solitude.
The house enrages me.

I go miles, pushing the pram,
thinking about Christina Rossetti's
black dresses – my own absent poems.

I go miles, touching his blankets proudly,
drawing the quilt to his lips.

I write of winter and the approaches to winter.
Air clings to me, rotten Lord Derbies,
patched in their skins, thud down.
The petals of Michaelmas daisies give light.

Now I'm that glimpsed figure for children
occupying doorways and windows;
that breath of succulence
ignored till nightfall.

I go out before the curtains are drawn
and walk close to the windows
which shine secretly.
Bare to the street
red pleats of a lampshade expose
bodies in classic postures, arguing.

Their senseless jokes explode with saliva.
I mop and tousle.

It's three o'clock in the cul-de-sac.
Out of the reach of traffic,
free from the ply
of bodies glancing and crossing,
the shopping, visiting,
cashing orders at the post office,

I lie on my bed in the sun
drawing down streams of babble.
This room holds me, a dull
round bulb stubbornly
rising year after year in the same place.

The night chemist

In the chemist's at night-time
swathed counters and lights turned down
lean and surround us.

Waiting for our prescriptions
we clock these sounds:
a baby's peaked hush,
hawked breath.

I pay a pound
and pills fall in my curled palms.
Holding their white packages tenderly
patients track back to the pain.

'Why is the man shouting?' Oliver asks me.
I answer, 'He wants to go home.'
Softly, muffled by cloth
the words still come
and the red-streaked drunkard goes past us,
rage scalding us.

I would not dare bring happiness
into the chemist's at night-time.
Its gift-wrapped lack of assistance still presses
as suffering closes the blinded windows.

St Paul's

This evening clouds darken the street quickly,
more and more grey
flows through the yellowing treetops,

traffic flies downhill
roaring and spangled with faces,
full buses
rock past the Sussex Place roundabout.

In Sussex the line of Downs
has no trees to uncover,
no lick of the town's wealth, blue
in smoke, no gold, fugitive dropping.
In villages old England
checks rainfall, sick of itself.

Here there are scraps and flashes:
bellying food smells – last minute buying –
plantain, quarters of ham.
The bread shop lady pulls down
loaves that will make tomorrow's cheap line.

On offer are toothpaste and shoe soles
mended same day for Monday's interview
and a precise network of choices
for old women collecting their pension
on Thursday, already owing the rent man.

Some places are boarded. You lose your expectancy –
soon it appears you never get home. Still
it's fine on evenings and in October
to settle here. Still the lights splashing look beautiful.

Poem for December 28

My nephews with almond faces
black hair like bunches of grapes

    (the skin stroked and then bruised
    the head buried and caressed)

he takes his son's head in his hands
kisses it   blesses it   leaves it:

the boy with circles under his eyes like damsons
not the blond baby, the stepson.

In the forest stories about the black
father   the jew   the incubus

if there are more curses they fall on us.

Behind the swinging ropes of their isolation
my nephews wait, sucking their sweets.
The hall fills quickly and neatly.

If they keep still as water
  I'll know them.
I look but I can't be certain:

my nephews with heavy eyelids
blowing in the last touches of daylight

my sisters raising them up like torches.

Greenham Common

Today is barred with darkness of winter.
In cold tents women protest,
for once unveiled, eyes stinging with smoke.

They stamp round fires in quilted anoraks,
glamourless, they laugh often
and teach themselves to speak eloquently.
Mud and the camp's raw bones
set them before the television camera.

Absent, the women of old photographs
holding the last of their four children,
eyes darkened, hair covered,
bodies waxy as cyclamen;
absent, all these suffering ones.

New voices rip at the throat,
new costumes, metamorphoses.

Soft-skirted, evasive
women were drawn from the ruins,
swirls of ash on them like veils.

History came as a seducer
and said: this is the beauty of women
in bombfall. Dolorous
you curl your skirts over your sleeping children.

Instead they stay at this place
all winter; eat from packets and jars,
keep sensible, don't hunger,
battle each day at the wires.

Poem for hidden women

'Fuck this staring paper and table –
I've just about had enough of it.

I'm going out for some air,'
he says, letting the wind bang up his sheets of poems.

He walks quickly; it's cool,
and rainy sky covers both stars and moon.
Out of the windows come slight
echoes of conversations receding upstairs.

There. He slows down.
A dark side-street – thick bushes –
he doesn't see them.
He smokes. Leaves can stir as they please.

(We clack like jackrabbits from pool to pool of lamplight.
Stretching our lips, we walk exposed
as milk cattle past heaps of rubbish

killed by the edge
of knowledge that trees hide
a face slowly detaching itself
from shadow, and starting to smile.)

The poet goes into the steep alleys
close to the sea, where fish scales line the gutter
and women prostitute themselves to men
as men have described in many poems.

They've said how milky, or bitter
as lemons they find her –
the smell of her hair
...vanilla...cinnamon...
there's a smell for every complexion.

Cavafy tells us he went always
to secret rooms and purer vices;
he wished to dissociate himself
from the hasty unlacings of citizens
fumbling, capsizing –
white
flesh in a mound and kept from sight,

but he doesn't tell us
whether these boys' hair always smelled of cinnamon
or if their nights cost more than spices.

A woman goes into the night café,
chooses a clean
knife and a spoon
and takes up her tray.
Quickly the manageress leans from the counter.
(As when a policeman arrests a friend
her eyes plunge and her voice roughens.)
She points to a notice with her red nail:
'After 11 we serve only accompanied females.'

The woman fumbles her grip
on her bag, and it slips.
Her forces tumble.
People look on as she scrabbles
for money and tampax.
A thousand shadows accompany her
down the stiff lino, through the street lighting.

The poet sits in a harbour bar
where the tables are smooth and solid to lean on.
It's peaceful. Men gaze
for hours at beer and brass glistening.
The sea laps. The door swings.

The poet feels poems
invade him. All day he has been stone-breaking
he says. He would be happier in cafés
in other countries, drinking, watching;

he feels he's a familiar sort of poet
but he's at ease with it.
Besides, he's not actually writing a poem:
there's plenty, he's sure,
in drink and hearing the sea move.

For what is Emily Dickinson doing
back at the house – the home?
A doctor emerges, wiping his face,
and pins a notice on the porch.
After a while you don't even ask.

No history
gets at this picture:
a woman named Sappho
sat in bars by purple water
with her feet crossed at the ankles
and her hair flaming with violets
never smiling when she didn't feel like it.

'End here, it's hopeful,'
says the poet, getting up from the table.

If no revolution come

If no revolution come
star clusters
will brush heavy on the sky

and grapes burst
into the mouths of fifteen
well-fed men,

these honest men
will build them houses like pork palaces
if no revolution come,

short-life dust children
will be crumbling in the sun –
they have to score like this
if no revolution come.

The sadness of people
don't look at it too long:
you're studying for madness
if no revolution come.

If no revolution come
it will be born sleeping,
it will be heavy as baby
playing on mama's bones,

it will be gun-thumping on Sunday
and easy good time
for men who make money,

for men who make money
grow like a roof
so the rubbish of people
can't live underneath.

If no revolution come
star clusters
will drop heavy from the sky

and blood burst
out of the mouths of fifteen
washing women,

and the land-owners will drink us
one body by one:
they have to score like this
if no revolution come.

A safe light

I hung up the sheets in moonlight,
surprised that it really was so
steady, a quickly moving pencil

flowing onto the stained cotton.
How the valves
in that map
of taut fabric
blew in and blew out

then spread flat
over the tiles
while the moon filled them with light.

A hundred feet above the town
for once the moonscape showed nothing extraordinary

only the clicking pegs
and radio news from our kitchen.
One moth hesitated
tapping at our lighted window

and in the same way the moonlight
covered the streets, all night.

Near Dawlish

Her fast asleep face turns from me,
the oil on her eyelids gleams
and the shadow of a removed moustache
darkens the curve of her mouth,

her lips are still flattened together
and years occupy her face,
her holiday embroidery glistens,
her fingers quiver then rest.

I perch in my pink dress
sleepiness fanning my cheeks,
not lurching, not touching
as the train leaps.

Mother, you should not be sleeping.
Look how dirty my face is, and lick
the smuts off me with your salt spit.

Golden corn rocks to the window
as the train jerks. Your narrowing body leaves me
frightened, too frightened to cry for you.

The last day of the exhausted month

The last day of the exhausted month
of August. Hydrangeas
purple and white like flesh immersed in water
with no shine
to keep the air off them
open their tepid petals more and more widely.

The newly-poured tar smells antiseptic
like sheets moulding on feverish skin:
surfaces of bedrock, glasslike passivity.

The last day of the exhausted month
goes quickly. A brown parcel
arrives with clothes left at the summer lodgings,
split and too small.
A dog noses
better not look at it too closely
God knows why they bothered to send them at all.

A smell of cat
joins us just before eating.

The cat is dead but its brown
smell still seeps from my tub of roses.

Harvest festival

Rain stands off, this still morning.
Gary and Matthew bring sheaves
of stick beans out of the allotment,

Lisa comes running, late,
with two sprays of Michaelmas daisies.
I put them in the green jar
next to yesterday's branch of fuchsia.

Strange how precise and exotic they are
close to –
I pass a dozen dun-coloured gardens
walking to school.

The separate red lines of housing trail
over the hill
at the end of the day two children
dragging a pram
look in the hedges for privet-moth caterpillar.

Close, they gaze at its stripes,
their pale heads similar, down-looking,

and frown, touching its back gently
as they have sometimes touched the fuchsia petals.

Second marriages

These second marriages arching within
smiles of their former friends:
his former wife and her child-swapping
remnants of weekday companionship,
her former husband, his regular
friends who encircled her
those wet Saturdays after the baby was born.

The children's early birthdays, the tea
and talk about socialisation;
the shared potties.
Frozen in these is the father's
morning exit from the maternity hospital.

Sliced from the album those gowns
that blood; the shawl in a heap,
those marital triumphant
glances at night when they got him to sleep.

Second marriages endure without these
public and early successes,
no longer tempting others or fate
by their caresses.

The deserted table

Coiled peel goes soft on the deserted table
where faïence, bubble glasses, and the rest
of riches thicken.

People have left their bread and potatoes.
Each evening baskets
of broken dinner hit the disposal unit.

Four children, product of two marriages,
two wives, countless slighter relations
and friends all come to the table

bringing new wines discovered on holiday,
fresh thirtyish faces, the chopped
Japanese dip of perfectly nourished hairstyles,
more children, more confident voices,
wave after wave consuming the table.

The writer's son

The father is a writer; the son
(almost incapable of speech)
explores him.

'Why did you take my language
my childhood
my body all sand?

why did you gather my movements
waves pouncing
eyes steering me till I crumbled?

We're riveted. I'm in the house
hung up with verbiage like nets.
A patchwork monster at the desk
bending the keys of your electric typewriters.

You're best at talking. I know
your hesitant, plain vowels.
Your boy's voice, blurred,
passed through my cot bars, stealing my baby magic.
You were the one they smiled at.'

Ollie and Charles at St Andrew's Park

Up at the park once more
the afternoon ends.
My sister and I huddle in quilted jackets.

A cigarette burn
crinkles the pushchair waterproofs,
the baby relaxes
sucking his hood's curled edges.

Still out of breath
from shoving and easing the wheels
on broken pavement we stay here.
Daffodils break in the wintry bushes

and Ollie and Charles in drab parkas
run, letting us wait by the swings.
Under eskimo hoods their hair springs
dun coloured, child-smelling.

They squat, and we speak quietly,
occasionally scanning the indigo patched
shadows with children melted against them.

Winter fairs

The winter fairs are all over.
The smells of coffee and naphtha
thin and are quite gone.

An orange tossed in the air
hung like a wonder
everyone would catch once,

the children's excitable cheeks
and woollen caps that they wore
tight, up to the ears,
are all quietened, disbudded;

now am I walking the streets
noting a bit of gold paper? –
a curl of peel suggesting the whole
aromatic globe in the air.

In a wood near Turku

The summer cabins are padlocked.
Their smell of sandshoes
evaporates over the lake water
leaving pine walls to shoulder the ice.

Resin seals them in hard splashes.
The woodman
knocks at their sapless branches.

He gets sweet puffballs
and chanterelles in his jacket,
strips off fungus like yellow leather,
thumbs it, then hacks the tree trunk.

Hazy and cold as summer dawn
the day goes on,

wood rustles on wood,
close, as the mist thins
like smoke around the top of the pine trees
and once more the saw whines.

Landscape from the Monet Exhibition at Cardiff

My train halts in the snowfilled station.
Gauges tick and then cease
on ice as the track settles
and iron-bound rolling stock creaks.

Two work-people
walk up alongside us,
wool-wadded, shifting their picks,

the sun, small as a rose,
buds there in the distance.
The gangs throw handfuls of salt like sowers
and light fires to keep the points moving.

Here are trees, made with two strokes.
A lady with a tray of white teacups
walks lifting steam from window to window.

I'd like to pull down the sash and stay
here in the blue where it's still work time.
The hills smell cold and are far away
at standstill, where lamps bloom.

Breakfast

Often when the bread tin is empty
and there's no more money for the fire
I think of you, and the breakfast you laid for me
– black bread and honey and beer.

I threw out a panful of wine yesterday –
the aluminium had turned it sour –
I have two colours of bread to choose from,
I'd take the white if I were poor,

so indigence is distant as my hands
stiff in unheated washing water,
but you, with your generous gift of butter
and cheese with poppy seeds, all in one morning meal

have drawn the blinds up at the bedside window
and I can watch the ships' tall masts appear.

FROM **THE SEA SKATER**

(1986)

The bride's nights in a strange village

At three in the morning
while mist limps between houses
while cloaks and blankets
dampen with dew

the bride sleeps with her husband
bundled in a red blanket,
her mouth parts and a bubble
of sour breathing goes free.
She humps wool up to her ears
while her husband tightens his arms
and rocks her, mumbling. Neither awakes.

In the second month of the marriage
the bride wakes after midnight.
Damp-bodied
she lunges from sleep
hair pricking with sweat
breath knocking her sides.
She eels from her husband's grip
and crouches, listening.

The night is enlarged by sounds.
The rain has started.
It threshes leaves secretively
and there in the blackness
of whining dogs it finds out the house.
Its hiss enfolds her, blots up
her skin, then sifts off, whispering
in her like mirrors
the length of the rainy village.

Lazarus

Dumb, his lips swathed,
lips peaceful and dry

out of the swash and backwash of speech,

his face bound with a napkin,
his arms and his legs with gravecloths
in glistening daylight,

in dumbness, silky as flints
packed into chalk cliffs.

The age of the iron man
finished, the age of the stone
still blooming. Here are the avenues,
peaceful avenues with stone petals.

Here is a red-veined marble, and there
the white Carrara with black tracing

and all the messages, the pollen
on which passers-by hang, bee-like,

words joined onto words.

Dumb, his lips sealed
with mouth-to-mouth breathing,

he abhors earth music:
the midday, dwindling
shadow of requiems.

A life-size statue of limestone,
scaly and worn over nostril
and lip-arches,

with yellow lichen and snails
poured into his eyes.

Liquid oboe pulsations
trail him, but dumbly
he pedals his stone body onward

past slab after word-covered slab
towards the expressionless sea he loves best,

to Bethsaida from Bethany.

Christmas roses

I remember years ago, that we had Christmas roses:
cold, greeny things under the snow –
fantastic hellebores, harbingers
of the century's worst winter.

On little fields stitched over with drystone
we broke snow curds, our sledge
tossing us out at the wall.

For twelve years a plateau of sea
stopped at my parents' window.
Here the slow Flatholm foghorn
sucking at the house fabric

recalls my little month-old brother,
kept in the house for weeks
while those snow days piled up like plates
to an impossible tower.

They were building the match factory
to serve moors seeded with conifers
that year of the Bay of Pigs,

the year of Cuba, when adults muttered
of taking to the moors with a shotgun
when the bomb dropped.

Such conversation, rapaciously
stored in a nine year old's memory
breeds when I stare down Bridgwater Bay
to that glassy CEGB elegance, Hinkley
Point, treating the landscape like snow,
melting down marshes and long, lost
muddy horizons.

Fir thickets replace those cushions
of scratchy heather, and prick out the noise
of larks in the air, so constant
I never knew what it was.

Little hellebores with green veins,
not at all tender, and scentless
on frosty ground, with your own small
melt, your engine of growth:
that was the way I liked you.

I imagine you sent back from Africa

I imagine you sent back from Africa
leaving a patchwork of rust and khaki
sand silt in your tea and your blood.

The metal of tanks and cans
puckers your taste-buds.
Your tongue jumps from the touch
of charge left in a dying battery.

You spread your cards in the shade
of roving lorries whose canvas
tents twenty soldiers.
The greased cards patter
in chosen spaces.

I imagine you sent back from Africa
with a tin mug kept for the bullet hole
in at one angle and out another.

You mount the train at the port
asking if anywhere on earth
offers such grey, mild people.

Someone draws down the blind.
You see his buttons, his wrist,
his teeth filled to the roots.
He weakens the sunlight for you
and keeps watch on your face.
Your day sinks in a hollow of sleep
racket and megaphoned voices.

The troop-ship booms once. Laden
with new men she moves down the Sound
low in the water, egg-carrying.

But for you daylight
with your relieved breath
supping up train dirt.
A jolt is a rescue from sleep
and a glaze of filth from the arm-rest
patches your cheek. You try to catch voices
calling out stations closer to home.

The knight

In the dusk of a forest chapel
a knight lies bleeding.

The edges of his wound are rawly
exhausted by blood chafing
but still the blood gathers and wells.

At first he lay with his arms folded
waiting for his brother officers
his dog curled at his feet,

but soon the dog with a whimper
made off, tearing its fur,
and soon the knight, moaning,
tried to cuddle into a foetal position
but the terrible wound prevented him.

His armour has become a bandage
as stiff as the casing of a chrysalis.
His face no longer has the strength for amazement.

The knight cries for his mother
in the dark of a forest chapel.
He wants the smell of her
and of all living things
which are not bleeding.

The scent and hissing of pine needles
make him believe he's in a hospital
where nurses pass by him.
He is afraid of falling
and of the stone floor under him.

In the dusk of a forest chapel
a knight lies bleeding.
In search of comfort
he turns to the warmer
grain of the wooden
bench he lies on
and licks its salty
whorls with his tongue.

In memoriam Cyril Smith 1913-1945

I've approached him since childhood,
since he was old, blurred,

my stake in the playground chants
and war games,

a word like 'brother'
mixed with a death story.

Wearing shorts and a smile
he stayed in the photograph box.

His hair was receding early.
He had Grandpa's long lip and my mother's love.

The jungle obliterates a city
of cries and murmurs,
bloody discharges
and unsent telegrams.

Now he is immanent

breaking off thoughts

printing that roll of film
one sweaty evening.

Four decades
have raised a thicket of deaths around him

a fence of thorn and a fence of roses.

His mother, my grandmother,
his father, his brother,

his camp companions

his one postcard.

The circle closes
in skin, limbs
and new resemblances.

We wanted to bring him
through life with us

but he grows younger.

We've passed him
holding out arms.

The parachute packers

The parachute packers with white faces
swathed over with sleep
and the stale bodily smell of sheets

make haste to tin huts where a twelve-hour
shift starts in ten minutes.
Their bare legs pump bicycle pedals,
they clatter on wooden-soled sandals
into the dazzling light over the work benches.

They rub in today's issue of hand-cream.
Their fingers skim on the silk
as the unwieldy billows of parachute flatten
like sea-waves, oiled, folded in sevens.

The only silk to be had
comes in a military packaging:
dull-green, printed, discreet,
gone into fashioning parachutes
to be wondered at like the flowers'
down-spinning, seed-bearing canopies
lodged in the silt of village memory.

A girl pulling swedes in a field
senses the shadow of parachutes
and gapes up, knees braced
and hair tangling. She must be riddled,
her warm juices all spilled
for looking upwards too early
into the dawn, leafy with parachutes.

Heavenly wide canopies
bring down stolid chaps with their rifle butts
ready to crack, with papers
to govern the upturned land,
with boots, barbed wire and lists on fine paper
thousands of names long.

I look up now at two seagulls,
at cloud drifts and a lamp-post
bent like a feeding swan,

and at the sound of needles
seaming up parachutes in Nissen huts
with a hiss and pull through the stuff
of these celestial ball-dresses

for nuns, agents, snow-on-the-boots men
sewn into a flower's corolla
to the music of Workers' Playtime.

At dusk the parachute packers
release their hair from its nets
and ride down lanes whitened by cow-parsley
to village halls, where the dances
and beer and the first cigarettes
expunge the clouds of parachute silk
and rules touching their hair and flesh.

In the bar they're the girls who pack parachutes
for our boys. They can forget
the coughs of the guard on duty,
the boredom and long hours
and half-heard cries of caught parachutists.

Porpoise washed up on the beach

After midday the great lazy
slaps of the sea,
the whistling of a boy who likes the empty
hour while the beach is feeding,

the cliffs vacant, gulls untidily drowsing
far out on the water.

I walked on in the dazzle
round to the next cove
where the sea was running backwards like mercury
from people busy at cutting
windows in the side of a beached porpoise.

The creature had died recently.
Naturally its blood was mammalian,
its skin supple and tough; it made me
instantly think of uses for it –
shoe soling, sealing the hulls of boats –
something to explain the intent knives
and people swiftly looking at me.

But there was no mussel harvest on the rocks
or boat blinding through noon
out to the crab pots,
not here but elsewhere the settled
stupor of digestion went on.

The porpoise had brought the boys between fourteen and eighteen,
lengthened their lives by a burning
profitless noon-time,
so they cut windows out of surprise
or idleness, finding the thing here
like a blank wall, inviting them.

They jumped from its body, prodded it,
looked in its mouth and its eyes,
hauled up its tail like a child's drawing
and became serious.

Each had the use of the knife in turn
and paused over the usual graffiti
to test words first with a knife-point
and fit the grey boulder of flesh under them.

Clapping their wings the gulls came back from the sea,
the pink screens of the hotel opened,
the last boy scoured the knife with sand.

I walked back along the shingle
breathing away the bloody trail of the porpoise
and saw the boys' wet heads glittering,
their hooting, diving
bodies sweeping them out of the bay.

In deep water

For three years I've been wary of deep water.
I busied myself on the shore
towelling, handing out underwear,
wading the baby knee-high.

I didn't think I had forgotten
how to play in the deep water,
but it was only today I went there
passing the paddle boats and bathers,
the parallel harbour wall,
until there was no one at all but me
rolling through the cold water
and scarcely bothering to swim
from pure buoyancy.

Of course I could still see them:
the red and the orange armbands,
the man smiling and pointing seawards,
the tender faces.

It's these faces that have taken me
out of the deep water
and made my face clench like my mother's
once, as I pranced on a ten-foot
wall over a glass-house.

The water remembers my body,
stretched and paler as it is.
Down there is my old reflection
spread-eagled, steadily moving.

Lady Macduff and the primroses

Now the snowdrop, the wood-anemone, the crocus
have flowered
and faded back to dry, scarcely-seen threads,

Lady Macduff goes down to the meadow
where primrose flowers are thickening.

Her maid told her this morning, It's time
to pick them now, there will never be more
without some dying.

Even the kitchen girls, spared for an hour,
come to pick flowers for wine.

The children's nurse has never seemed to grasp
that she only need lay down the flowers loosely,

the flat-bottomed baskets soon fill
with yellow, chill primroses covered by sturdy leaves,

but the nurse will weave posies
even though the children are impatient
and only care who is first, has most
of their mother's quick smile.

Pasties have been brought from the castle.
Savoury juices spill from their ornate crusts,
white cloths are smeared with venison gravy
and all eat hungrily
out in the spring wind.

Lady Macduff looks round at the sparkling
sharpness of grass, whipped kerchiefs and castle battlements
edged with green light

and the primroses like a fall
colder than rain, warmer than snow,
petals quite still, hairy stems helplessly curling.

She thinks how they will be drunk
as yellow wine, swallow by swallow
filling the pauses of mid-winter,
sweet to raw throats.

Mary Shelley

> *'No living poet ever arrived at the fulness of his fame; the jury which sits in judgement upon a poet, belonging as he does to all time, must be composed of his peers.'* (Percy Bysshe Shelley)

In the weightlessness of time and our passage within it
voices and rooms swim.
Cleft after soft cleft
parts, word-covered lips
thin as they speak.

I should recall how pink and tender
your lids looked when you read too long
while I produced seamed
patchwork, my own phantom.

Am I the jury, the evidence,
the recollection?

Last night I dreamed of a prospect
and so I dreamed backwards:

first I woke in the dark
scraping my knuckles on board and mould.

I remember half listening
or reading in the shadow of a fire;
each evening I would lie quietly
breathing the scent of my flesh till I slept.

I loved myself in my new dress.
I loved the coral stems rising from the rosebush
under my window in March.
I was intact, neat,
dressing myself each morning.

I dreamed my little baby was alive
mewing for me from somewhere in the room.
I chafed her feet and tucked her nightdress close.

Claire, Shelley and I left England.
We crossed the Channel and boasted afterwards
of soaked clothes, vomit and cloudbursts.

We went by grey houses, shutters still closed,
people warmly asleep. My eyes were dazed
wide open in abatement and vacancy.

*

'A bad wife is like winter in the house.'
(diary of Claire Clairmont, Florence 1820)

In Florence in winter grit scoured between houses;
the plaster needed replacing, the children had coughs.

I lived in a nursery which smelled of boredom and liniment.
In bed I used to dream of water crossings
by night. I looked fixedly forward.
It was the first winter I became ugly:
I was unloving all winter,
frozen by my own omens.

In Lerici I watched small boats on the bay
trace their insect trails on the flat water.
Orange lamps and orange blossom
lit and suffused the night garden.

Canvas slashed in a squall.
Stifling tangles of sail and fragile
masts snapping brought the boat over.
The blackened sea
kept its waves still, then tilting
knocked you into its cold crevices.

I was pressed to a pinpoint,
my breath flat.
Scarcely pulsating
I gave out nothing.

I gave out nothing before your death.
We would pass in the house with blind-lipped
anger in me.
You put me aside for the winter.

I would soften like a season
I would moisten and turn to you.
I would not conform my arms to the shapes of dead children.

I patched my babies and fed them
but death got at them.
Your eyes fed everywhere.

I wonder at bodies once clustered,
at delicate tissue
emerging unable to ripen.

Each time I returned to life
calmer than the blood which left me
weightless as the ticking of a blind-cord.
Inside my amply-filled dress
I am renewed seamlessly.

Fledged in my widow's weeds
I was made over, for this
prickle of live flesh
wedged in its own corpulence.

The plum tree

The plum was my parents' tree,
above them
as I was at my bedroom window
wondering why they chose to walk this way quietly
under the plum tree.

My sisters and I stopped playing
as they reached up and felt for the fruit.
It lay among bunches of leaves,
oval and oozing resin
out into pearls of gum.
They bit into the plums
without once glancing
back at the house.

Some years were thin:
white mildew streaking the trunk,
fruit buckled and green,

but one April
the tree broke from its temperate blossoming
and by late summer the branches
trailed earth, heavy with pound
after pound of bursting Victorias,

and I remember the oblivious steps
my parents took as they went quietly
out of the house one summer evening
to stand under the plum tree.

The air-blue gown

Tonight I'm eating the past
consuming its traces,

the past is a heap
sparkling with razor blades
where patches of sweetness
deepen to compost,

woodlice fold up their legs
and roll luxuriously,

cold vegetation
rises to blood heat.

The local sea's bare
running up to the house

tufting its waves
with red seaweed
spread against a Hebridean noon.

Lightly as sandpipers marking the shoreline
boats at the jetty sprang
and rocked upon the green water.

Not much time passes, but suddenly
now when you're crumpled after a cold
I see how the scale and changes
of few words measure us.

At this time of year I remember a cuckoo's
erratic notes on a mild morning.
It lay full-fed on a cherry branch
repeating an hour of sweetness
its grey body unstirring
its lustrous eyes turning.

Talk sticks and patches
walls and the kitchen formica
while at the table outlines
seated on a thousand evenings
drain like light going out of a landscape.

The back door closes, swings shut,
drives me to place myself inside it.
In this flickering encampment
fire pours sideways
then once more stands
evenly burning.

I wake with a touch on my face
and turn sideways
butting my head into darkness.

The wind's banging diminishes. An aircraft
wanders through the upper atmosphere
bee-like, propelled by loneliness.
It searches for a fallen corolla,
its note rising and going
as it crosses the four quarters.

The city turns a seamed cheek upward,
confides itself to the sound and hazardous
construction of a journey by starlight.

I drop back soundlessly,
my lips slackened.
Headache alone is my navigator,
plummeting, shedding its petals.

It's Christmas Eve.
Against my nightdress a child's foot, burning,
passes its fever through the cotton,

the tide of bells swings
and the child winces.

The bells are shamelessly
clanging, the voices
hollering churchward.

I'm eating the past tonight
tasting gardenia perfume
licking the child-like socket of an acorn
before each is consumed.

It was not Hardy who stayed there
searching for the air-blue gown.
It was the woman who once more, secretly,
tried the dress on.

Doña Juanita and the male stickleback

At dawn Doña Juanita faces her mirror.
She watches a hawk dive on her fish ponds,
the dewy garden assume colour and form,
the golden carp swim for the daphnia.
A gardener whistles, swinging his can
to damp the walks of her maze.

Doña Juanita turns to the bed
and to the man sleeping.
She draws back the sheet
so that he stirs uneasily, feeling
the cooler air and himself revealed.

She walks into the garden
taking a basket of food for her fish,
and there they dart through the lilies and glide
to their habitual feeding-places,
eeling through wet stems and white-crowned
flowers which burst in the light.

Doña Juanita wishes to touch
the golden sides of her fish.
She lets her hands sink in the green pond
and weave with the water movement.
The fish nuzzle along her. They buck
their tense bodies and, mouths wide,
guzzle the crumbled egg-yolk she gives them.

Deep in the pond a male stickleback
makes his barrel-shaped nest in the silt
and glues it with his own juices.
Now, like an anxious late-marrying man
too ugly to mate easily,
he searches for females and chivvies them
into the nest with his sharp spines.

One by one they lay their burden of eggs
until the full nest rocks there, replete.

He squirts his horde over with milky semen
and settles to wait.
Now the nest shakes
in the current of passing predators
and the male stickleback guards
his hatching eggs, snapping at carp,
blindly glaring at pond debris,
duelling with dead leaves.

The fry emerge and he shelters
and chastens the teeming brood,
herding them back to safety,
letting them feed and play in the nest doorway.

After a month the young
outgrow his cherishing.
They swim off, snapping at weed,
forgetful at once of him.
Now the exhausted male stickleback
dies beside his collapsed nest
while the females of the great ponds
antic and feed in their depths.

Doña Juanita gathers her wet hem
and walks the paths with a hiss of skirts
under the mulberry whose black fruits
spatter the gravel beneath them.
At her desk in the summer-house
she sets out her documents.
Long lines of her black writing
unreel with scarcely a pause.
she deploys orchards and vineyards
and chides farmers for rent.

The garden trembles with heat.
its leaves moisten, its shadows
are brief pools.
The carp sink to the dark silt
depths of the ponds, and there, veiled
by brown clouds, torpid,
absorb the ground meat and the egg of the morning.

My sad descendants

O wintry ones, my sad descendants,
with snowdrops in your hands you join me
to celebrate these dark, short
days lacking a thread of sun.

Three is a virtuous number,
each time one fewer to love,
the number of fairy tales,
wishes, labours for love.

My sad descendants
who had no place in the sun,
hope brought you to mid-winter,
never to spring
or to the lazy benches of summer
and old bones.

My sad descendants
whose bones are a network of frost,
I carry your burn and your pallor,
your substance dwindled to drops.

I breathe you another pattern
since no breath warmed you from mine,
on the cold of the night window
I breathe you another pattern,

I make you outlive rosiness
and envied heartbeats.

Patrick at four years old on Bonfire Night

Cursing softly and letting the matches drop
too close to the firework box,
we light an oblation
to rough-scented autumnal gods,
shaggy as chrysanthemums;

and you, in your pearly maroon
waterproof suit, with your round
baby brows, stare upward and name
chrysanthemum fountain and silver fountain
and Catherine wheel: saints' names
like yours, Patrick, and you record them.
This morning, climbing up on my pillow,
you list saints' names guessed at from school.

They go off, one by one on the ritual plank:
jack-in-a-box, high-jump and Roman candle,
searching the currant bushes with gunpowder.

We stand in savoury fumes like pillars,
our coats dark, our slow-burning fuse lit,
and make our little bonfire with spits
for foil-wrapped potatoes and hot-dogs –

by your bedtime
the rough-scented autumnal gods
fuse with the saints and jack-lanterns.

The horse landscape

Today in a horse landscape
horses steam in the lee of thorn hedges
on soaking fields. Horses waltz
on iron poles in dank fairgrounds.

A girl in jodhpurs on Sand Bay
leads her pony over and over
jumps made of driftwood and traffic cones.

A TV blares the gabble of photofinishes.
The bookie's plastic curtain releases
punters onto the hot street
littered with King Cone papers.

In a landscape with clouds and chalk downs
and cream houses, a horse rigid as bone
glares up at kites and hang-gliders.

One eye's cut from the flowered turf:
a horse skull, whispering secrets
with wind-sighs like tapping on phone wires.

The group leader in beautiful boots
always on horse-back,
the mounted lady squinnying
down at the hunt intruders,
draw blood for their own horse landscape
and scorn horse-trading, letting the beasts mate
on scrubby fields, amongst catkins
and watery ditches.

Here's a rearing bronze horse
welded to man, letting his hands
stay free for banner and weapon –
mild shadow of Pushkin's nightmare.

Trained police horses sway on great hooves.
Riders avoid our faces, and gaze
down on our skull crowns
where the bone jigsaw cleaves.

Grooms whistle and urge
the sweaty beasts to endure battle.
We're always the poor infantry
backing off Mars field,
out of frame for the heroic riders
preserved in their horse landscape.

Thetis

Thetis, mother of all mothers
who fear the death of their children,
held down her baby Achilles
in the dark Styx

whose waters flow fast
without ripples or wave-break,
bearing little boats of paper
with matchstick masts,
returning not even a sigh
or drenched fibre to life.

Thetis, mother of all mothers
destined to outlive their children,
took Achilles by the heel
and thrust him into the Styx

so that sealed, immortal, dark-eyed,
he'd return to his white cradle
and to his willow rattle.

She might have held him less tightly
and for a while given him
wholly to the trustworthy river
which has no eddies or backwaters
and always carries its burdens onward,
she might have left him to play
on the soft grass of the river-edge.

But through the pressure-marks of her white fingers
the baby found his way forward
towards the wound he knew best.
Even while the arrow was in the wood
and the bow gleaming with leaves
the current of the Styx
faintly suckled and started
in the little flexed ankles
pressed against Thetis' damp breasts.

In the tents

Our day off, agreed by the wind
and miry fields and unburied dead,
in the tent with first light filtering
a rosy dawn which masks rain.

The rosiness rests on our damp flesh,
on armour stacked by the tent walls,
on our captain and his lolling companion.

I go down to the sea shore
to find white pebbles for games.
I look for the island, kidding myself
I see it hump through the waves.

Back in the tent it's warm, wine-smelling,
heavy with breath.
The lamp shines on the bodies
of our captain and his companion.

These are the tented days I remember
more than the battles.
This is the smell of a herbal rub
on great Achilles.
This is the blue soap-scum on the pitcher,
and cold parcels of goat-meat,
the yawning moment
late in the evening, when I step out
and see the stars alight in their same places.

Uncle Will's telegram

She kept Uncle Will's telegram
between the sheets of her wedding-album.
Her life-long imaginary future
dazzled the moment it came.

He tried the counter-top biro
and asked the post office clerk
to check the time of arrival
for ten words in block capitals.

In the levelled-down churchyard
they posed for the first photographs
while powdery grandmothers
whispered 'We wish you'
and came up with the word 'Happiness'.

She stood against laurel-black cherries
while the church dived into silence,
a great maritime creature
leaving without echoes.
At the lych-gate a tide-line
of white flowers remained.

In the Flowers the best man
read Uncle Will's telegram
and the guests lifted their glasses
shouting 'Io, Io Hymen!'

Rapunzel

Rapunzel
let down your hair,

let your strong hair
wind up the water you wish for.

All your life looking down
on bright tree-tops
your days go by quickly.

You read and you eat
in your white tower top
where sunlight fans through high
windows and far below you
bushes are matted with night.

With soft thumbprints
darkness muddles your pages.
The prince arrives,
whose noisy breathing
and sweat as he vaults your window-sill
draw you like wheat fields
on the enchanted horizontal.

He seeds your body with human fragments,
dandruff, nail-clippings, dust.
The detritus of new pleasures
falls on your waxed boards.

Your witch mother, sweeping them,
sorrowfully banishes the girl
who has let a prince clamber her.

For six years you wander the desert
from level to pale level.
At night you make a bunker to sleep in
near to the coyotes.

The ragged prince plays blind-man's-buff
to the sound of your voice singing
as you gather desert grasses
in hollows hidden from him.

Daily your wise mother
unpicks the walls of the tower.
Its stones are taken for sheep-folds,
your circle of hair
hidden beneath the brambles.

Bewick's swans

Ahead of us, moving through time
with a skein's precision and mystery
over the navy spaces of winter
the inter-continental migration continues.

It starts on one moment
of one season, when time ripens
down to the soft dawn chill on a feather

or the germ sprouting in winter wheat
ready to be grazed by the wild swans.

Hour by hour the birds move up the wedge
until they fly at its point, in the keen
apex, the buffet of wind.
A dark triangle of birds streams backward
and peels away and reforms like rain on glass.

Sometimes they fall almost to the white waves
then stretch their necks and call and begin
the long pull onward, leaving a swan plunged
like an untidy bundle of sheets
swept in a ship's backwash.

See them nose the long coastline
in a glide of perfected instinct.
To their preferred feeding-grounds
they are a long arrow
shot from unimaginable nowhere.
Here they are keeled, treading
the known roughness of grass tussocks.

The private swans arch out their feathers
and preen and nourish themselves.
The mild floodlights each night
and people gathered to watch
are no stranger to the swans than the prickle
of green waiting in the wheat stripes each winter.

The sea skater

A skater comes to this blue pond,
his worn Canadian skates
held by the straps.

He sits on the grass
lacing stiff boots
into a wreath of effort and breath.

He tugs at the straps and they sound
as ice does when weight troubles it
and cracks bloom around stones

creaking in quiet mid-winter
mid-afternoons: a fine time for a skater.
He knows it and gauges the sun
to see how long it will be safe to skate.

Now he hisses and spins in jumps
while powder ice clings to the air
but by trade he's a long-haul skater.

Little villages, stick-like in the cold,
offer a child or a farm-worker
going his round. These watch him
go beating onward between iced alders
seawards, and so they picture him
always smoothly facing forward, foodless and waterless,
mounting the crusted waves on his skates.

In the tea house

In the tea house the usual
customers sit with their cooling
tea glasses
and new pastries
sealed at the edge
with sticky droplets.

The waitress walks off,
calves solid and shapely as vases,
leaving a juicy baba
before her favourite.

Each table has bronze or white chrysanthemums
and the copper glass-stands imperceptibly
brush each other like crickets
suddenly focussed at dusk,

but the daily newspapers
dampened by steam
don't rustle.

The tea house still has its blinds out
even though the sun is now amiably
yellow as butter

and people hurrying by raise up their faces
without abandon, briskly
talking to their companions;

no one sits out at the tables
except a travel-stained couple
thumbing a map.

The waitress reckons her cloths
watching the proprietor
while he, dark-suited, buoyant,
pauses before a customer.

Her gaze breaks upon the tea-house
like incoming water
joining sandbanks swiftly and
softly moving the pebbles,

moving the coloured sugar and coffee
to better places,
counting the pastries.

Florence in permafrost

Cold pinches the hills around Florence.
It roots out vines, truffles for lemon trees
painfully heated by charcoal
to three degrees above freezing.

A bristling fir forest
moves forward over Tuscany.
A secret wood
riddled with worm and lifeless
dust-covered branches
stings the grass and makes it flowerless,

freezing the long-closed eyelids of Romans.
They sleep entrusted to darkness
in the perpetual, placid, waveless
music of darkness.

The forest ramps over frontiers and plains
and swallows voluble Customs men
in slow ash. A wind sound
scrapes its thatching of sticks.

Blind thrushes in the wood blunder
and drop onto the brown needles.
There are no nests or singing-places.

A forest of matchwood and cheap furniture
marches in rows. Nobody harvests
its spongey woods and makes the trunks sigh
like toy soldiers giving up life.

All over Italy and northward
from fair Florence to München
and the cold city of Potsdam
the forest spreads like a pelt
on meadows, terraces, riverbanks
and the shards of brick houses.

It hides everywhere from everywhere
as each point of perspective
is gained by herds of resinous firs.

There may be human creatures
at nest in the root sockets.
They whicker words to each other
against the soughing of evergreens
while the great faces of reindeer
come grazing beside the Arno.

Geneva

City of burghers and freedom fighters,
city without hinterlands,

November burns bright
on the Rhone pouring down snow
over the city of walled-up fighters.

Next to the glassy leaders,
a statue of Zwingli,
next to the nugget of glass
in the heart, 'our country
free from the Empire'.

Bone, liver and lights
join at the sheer table.
Little cancerous atoms
burn bright.

City without hinterlands
imagining 1812
and the retreat from Moscow,

Geneva, gin-clear
city of burghers and freedom fighters,
whose army has flapped off
from the immortal mantelpiece
coated with good Genevese messages,

whose Swiss guards stand at the Holy See
holding our squeezed breath,

fill their hearts up with rain, their livers with rain,
streak their document cases with rain,

fill their borrowed households with raindrops and buckets,
sink their hearts in a river brimming with peppermint,

let washed gobbets of paper
flower in overflows,

let the scarred seams of their skins,
their ageing diseases, their birthmarks
wash them away, make rivers of them

with slow, broad drops on the hart's-tongue fern
and slow, broad drops on the wet leaves
of the city of burghers and freedom fighters –
gin-clear Geneva.

Missile launcher passing at night

The soft fields part in hedges, each
binds each, copse pleats
rib up the hillside.

Darkness is coming and grass
bends downward.
The cattle out all night
eat, knee-deep, invisible
unless a headlight arcs on their mild faces.

The night's damp fastens, droplet by droplet,
onto the animals.
They vibrate to the passing of a missile launcher
and stir
their patient eyelashes.

A blackbird
startled by floodlights
reproduces morning.

Cattle grids tremble and clang,
boots scrape
holly bursts against wet walls
lost at the moment of happening.

FROM THE RAW GARDEN

(1988)

Code-breaking in the Garden of Eden

The Raw Garden is a collection of closely-related poems, which are intended to speak to, through, and even over each other. The poems draw their full effect from their setting; they feed from each other, even when the link is as mild as an echo of phrasing or cadence.

It is now possible to insert new genes into a chromosomal pattern. It is possible to feed in new genetic material, or to remove what is seen as faulty or damaged material. The basic genetic code is contained in DNA (deoxyribonucleic acid), and its molecular structure is the famous double helix, so called because it consists of two complementary spirals which match each other like the halves of a zip. Naturally-occurring enzymes can be used to split the double strand, and to insert new material. The separate strands are then recombined to form the complete DNA helix. By this process of gene-splicing a new piece of genetic information can be inserted into a living organism, and can be transmitted to the descendants of the organism.

It seems to me that there is an echo of this new and revolutionary scientific process in the way each poet feeds from the material drawn together in a long poetic tradition, "breaks" it with his or her individual creative voice, and recombines it through new poems.

One thing I have tried to do in these poems is to explore the effect which these new possibilities of genetic manipulation may have on our concept of what is natural and what is unnatural. If we can not follow Romantic poets in their assumption of a massive, unmalleable landscape which moulds the human creatures living upon it and provides them with a constant, stable frame of reference, then how do we look at landscape and at the "natural"? We are used to living in a profoundly human-made landscape. As I grew up I realised that even such apparently wild places as moors and commons were the product of human decisions and work: people had cut down trees, grazed animals, acquired legal rights. But still this knowledge did not interfere with my sense that these places were natural.

The question might be, what does it take to disturb the sense of naturalness held by the human being in his or her landscape? Is there a threshold beyond which a person revolts at a feeling that changedness has gone too far? Many of these poems focus on highly manipulated landscapes and outcrops of "nature", and on the harmonies and revulsions formed between them and the people living among them.

Perhaps the Garden of Eden embodies some yearning to print down an idea of the static and the predictable over our knowledge that we have to accept perpetual changeability. The code of the Garden of Eden has been broken open an infinite number of times. Now we are faced with a still greater potential for change, since we have acquired knowledge of the double helix structure of DNA. If the Garden of Eden really exists it does so moment by moment, fragmented and tough, cropping up like a fan of buddleia high up in the gutter of a deserted warehouse, or in a heap of frozen cabbages becoming luminous in the reflected light off roadside snow. This Garden of Eden propagates itself in strange ways, some of which find parallels in far-fetched horticultural techniques such as air layering, or growing potatoes in a mulch of rotted seaweed on white sand. I hope that these poems do not seem to hanker back to a prelapsarian state of grace. If I want to celebrate anything, it is resilience, adaptability, and the power of improvisation.

Seal run

The potatoes come out of the earth bright
as if waxed, shucking their compost,

and bob against the palm of my hand
like the blunt muzzles of seals swimming.

Slippy and pale in the washing-up bowl
they bask, playful, grown plump
in banks of seaweed on white sand,

seaweed hauled from brown circles
set in transparent waters off Easdale

all through the sun-fanned West Highland midnights
when the little potatoes are seeding there
to make necklaces under the mulch,
torques and amulets in their burial place.

The seals quiver, backstroking
for pure joy of it, down to the tidal
slim mouth of the loch,

they draw their lips back, their blunt whiskers
tingle at the inspout of salt water

then broaching the current they roll
off between islands and circles of oarweed.

At noon the sea-farmer
turns back his blanket of weed
and picks up potatoes like eggs
from their fly-swarming nest,

too fine for the sacks, so he puts them in boxes
and once there they smell earthy.

At noon the seals nose up the rocks
to pile there, sun-dazed,
back against belly, island on island.

and sleep, shivering like dogs
against the tug of the stream
flowing on south past Campbelltown.

The man's hands rummage about still
to find what is full-grown there.
Masts on the opposite shore ring faintly

disturbing themselves, and make him look up.
Hands down and still moving
he works on, his fingers at play blinded,
his gaze roving the ripe sea-loch.

Wild strawberries

What I get I bring home to you:
a dark handful, sweet-edged,
dissolving in one mouthful.

I bother to bring them for you
though they're so quickly over,
pulpless, sliding to juice,

a grainy rub on the tongue
and the taste's gone. If you remember
we were in the woods at wild strawberry time

and I was making a basket of dockleaves
to hold what you'd picked,
but the cold leaves unplaited themselves

and slid apart, and again unplaited themselves
until I gave up and ate wild strawberries
out of your hands for sweetness.

I lipped at your palm –
the little salt edge there,
the tang of money you'd handled.

As we stayed in the wood, hidden,
we heard the sound system below us
calling the winners at Chepstow,
faint as the breeze turned.

The sun came out on us, the shade blotches
went hazel: we heard names
bubble like stock-doves over the woods

as jockeys in stained silks gentled
those sweat-dark, shuddering horses
down to the walk.

A mortgage on a pear tree

A pear tree stands in its own maze.
It does not close its blossom all night
but holds out branchfuls of cool
wide-open flowers. Its slim leaves look black
and stir like tongues in the lamp-light.

It was here before the houses were built.
The owner grew wasteland and waited for values to rise.
The builders swerved a boundary sideways
to cup the tree in a garden. When they piled rubble
it was a soft cairn mounting the bole.

The first owner of the raw garden
came out and walked on the clay clods.
There was the pear tree, bent down
with small blunt fruits, each wide where the flower was,
shaped like a medlar, but sweet.

The ground was dense with fermenting pears,
half trodden to pulp, half eaten.
She could not walk without slipping.

Slowly she walked in her own maze,
sleepy, feeling the blood seep
down her cold fingers, down the spread branch
of veins which trails to the heart,

and remembered how she'd stood under a tree
holding out arms, with two school-friends.
It was the fainting-game,
played in the dinner-hour from pure boredom,
never recalled since. For years this was growing
to meet her, and now she's signed for her own
long mortgage over the pear tree
and is the gainer of its accrued beauty,

but when she goes into her bedroom
and draws her curtains against a spring night
the pear tree does not close its white blossom.
The flowers stay open with slim leaves flickering around them:
touched and used, they bear fruit.

A pæony truss on Sussex Place

Restless, the pæony truss tosses about
in a destructive spring wind.
Already its inner petals are white
without one moment of sun-warmed expansion.

The whole bunch of the thing looks poor
as a stout bare-legged woman in November
slopping her mules over the post office step
to cash a slip of her order book.

The wind rips round the announced site
for inner city conversion: this is the last tough
bit of the garden, with one lilac
half sheared-off and half blooming.

The AIDS ad is defaced and the Australian
lager-bright billboard smirks down
on wind-shrivelled passers-by who stayed put
to vote in the third Thatcher election.

The porch of the Elim Pentecostal Church brightens
as a woman in crimson and white suit
steps out, pins her hat down
then grasps the hands of her wind-tugged grandchildren.

Permafrost

For all frozen things –
my middle finger that whitens
from its old, ten-minute frostbite,

for black, slimy potatoes
left in the clamp,
for darkness and cold like cloths
over the cage,

for permafrost, lichen crusts
nuzzled by reindeer,
the tender balance of decades
null as a vault.

For all frozen things –
the princess and princes
staring out of their bunker
at the original wind,

for NATO survivors in nuclear moonsuits
whirled from continent to continent

like Okies in bumpy Fords
fleeing the dustbowl.

For all frozen things –
snowdrops and Christmas roses
blasted down to the germ
of their genetic zip-code.

They fly by memory –
cargo of endless winter,
clods of celeriac, chipped
turnips, lanterns at ten a.m.

in the gloom of a Finnish market-place;
flowers under glass, herring,
little wizened apples.

For all frozen things –
the nipped fish in a mess of ice,
the uncovered galleon
tossed from four centuries of memory,

for nuclear snowsuits bouncing on dust,
trapped on the rough ride of the earth's surface,
on the rough swing of its axis,

like moon-men lost on the moon
watching the earth's green flush

tremble and perish.

At Cabourg

Later my stepson will uncover a five-inch live shell
from a silted pool on the beach at St Côme. It is complete
with brass cap and a date on it: nineteen forty-three.
We'll look it up in the dictionary, take it
to show at the Musée de la Libération
– ce petit obus – but once they unwrap it
they'll drop the polite questions and scramble
full tilt for the Gendarmerie opposite.
The gendarmes will peer through its cradle of polythene
gingerly, laughing. One's at the phone
already – he gestures – 'Imagine! Let's tell them
we've got a live shell here in the Poste!'

Of course this will have happened before.
They'll have it exploded, there'll be no souvenir shell-case,
and we'll be left with our photographs
taken with a camera which turns out to be broken.

Later we'll be at the Château Fontaine-Henry
watching sleek daughters in jodhpurs come in from the fields.
I'll lie back in my green corduroy coat, and leave,
faint, to drive off through fields of sunflowers
without visiting the rooms we've paid for.
Madame will have her fausse-couche,
her intravenous injections, her glass ampoules,
in a room which is all bed
and smells of medicinal alcohol and fruit.
The children will play on the beach, a little forlornly,
in the wind which gusts up out of nowhere.

Later we'll see our friends on their lightweight bicycles
freewheeling tiredly downhill to Asnelles.
Their little son, propped up behind them
will glide past, silent, though he alone sees us.

But now we are on the beach at Cabourg,
stopped on our walk to look where the sky's whitening
over the sea beyond Dives. Now a child squawks
and races back as a wave slaps over his shorts' hem

to where a tanned woman with naked breasts
fidgets her baby's feet in the foam
straight down from the Boulevard Marcel Proust.

Ploughing the roughlands

It's not the four-wheeled drive crawler
spitting up dew and herbs,

not Dalapon followed by dressings
of dense phosphates,

nor ryegrass greening behind wire as behind glass,

not labourers wading in moonsuits
through mud gelded by paraquat –

but now, the sun-yellow, sky-blue
vehicles mount the pale chalk,

the sky bowls on the white hoops
and white breast of the roughland,

the farmer with Dutch eyes
guides forward the quick plough.

Now, flush after flush of Italian ryegrass
furs up the roughland

with its attentive, bright,
levelled-off growth –

pale monoculture
sweating off rivers of filth

fenced by the primary
colours of crawler and silo.

The land pensions

The land pensions, like rockets
shoot off from wheat with a soft yellow
flame-bulb: a rook or a man in black
flaps upwards with white messages.

On international mountains and spot markets
little commas of wheat translate.
The stony ground's pumped to a dense fire
by the flame-throwing of chemicals.
On stony ground the wheat can ignite
its long furls.

The soft rocket of land pensions flies
and is seen in Japan, covering
conical hills with its tender stars:
now it is firework time, remembrance
and melt-down of autumn chrysanthemums.

On bruised fields above Brighton
grey mould laces the wheat harvest.
The little rockets are black. Land pensions
fasten on silos elsewhere, far off.

Market men flicker and skulk like eels
half-way across earth to breed.
On thin chipped flint-and-bone land
a nitrate river laces the grey wheat
pensioning off chalk acres.

A dream of wool

Decoding a night's dreams
of sheepless uplands
the wool-merchant clings to the wool churches,

to trade with the Low Countries,
to profitable, downcast
ladies swathed in wool sleeves

whose plump, light-suffused faces
gaze from the triptychs he worships.

Sheep ticks, maggoty tails and foot-rot
enter his tally
of dense beasts, walking
with a winter's weight on their backs

through stubborn pasture
they graze to a hairsbreadth.

From the turf of the Fire Hills
the wool-merchant trawls
sheep for the marsh markets.
They fill mist with their thin cries –

circular eddies, bemusing
the buyers of mutton
from sheep too wretched to fleece.

In the right angle of morning sunshine
the aerial photographer
shoots from the blue,

decodes a landscape
of sheepless uplands
and ploughed drove roads,

decodes the airstream, the lapis lazuli
coat for many compacted skeletons
seaming the chalk by the sea.

New crops

O engines
flying over the light, barren
as shuttles, thrown over a huge
woof

crossply
of hedgeless snail tracks,
you are so high,

you've felled the damp crevices
you've felled the boulder-strewn meadow
the lichen
the strong plum tree.

O engines
swaying your rubber batons
on pods, on ripe lupins,
on a chameleon terrace
of greenlessness,

you're withdrawn from a sea
of harvests, you're the foreshore

of soaked soil leaching
undrinkable streams.

Shadows of my mother against a wall

The wood-pigeon rolls soft notes off its breast
in a tree which grows by a fence.
The smell of creosote,
easy as wild gum
oozing from tree boles
keeps me awake. A thunderstorm
heckles the air.

I step into a bedroom
pungent with child's sleep,
and lift the potty and pile of picture books
so my large shadow
crosses his eyes.

Sometimes at night, expectant,
I think I see the shadow of my mother
bridge a small house of enormous rooms.
Here are white, palpable walls
and stories of my grandmother:
the old hours of tenderness I missed.

Air layering

The rain was falling down in slow pulses
between the horse-chestnuts, as if it would set root there.

It was a slate-grey May evening
luminous with new leaves.
I was at a talk on the appearances of Our Lady
these past five years at Medjugorje.
We sat in a small room in the Presbytery:
the flow of the video scratched, the raindrop
brimmed its meniscus upon the window
from slant runnel to sill.

Later I watched a programme on air layering.
The round rootball steadied itself
high as a chaffinch nest, and then deftly
the gardener severed the new plant.
She knew its wounded stem would have made roots there.

The argument

It was too hot, that was the argument.
I had to walk a mile with my feet flaming
from brown sandals and sun.

Now the draggling shade of the privet made me to dawdle,
now soft tarmac had to be crossed.
I was lugging an old school-bag –

it was so hot the world was agape with it.
One limp rose fell as I passed.

An old witch sat in her front garden
under the spokes of a black umbrella
lashed to her kitchen chair.
God was in my feet as I fled past her.

Everyone I knew was so far away.
The yellow glob of my ice cream melted and spread.
I bought it with huge pennies, held up.
'A big one this time!' the man said,
so I ate on though it cloyed me.
It was for fetching the bread
one endless morning before Bank Holiday.

I was too young, that was the argument,
and had to propitiate everyone:
the man with the stroke, and the burnt lady
whose bared, magical teeth made me
smile if I could –
Oh the cowardice of my childhood!

The peach house

The dry glasshouse is almost empty.
A few pungent geraniums with lost markings
lean in their pots.

It is nothing but a cropping place for sun
on cold Northumbrian July days.

The little girl, fresh from suburbia,
cannot believe in the peaches she finds here.
They are green and furry as monkeys –
she picks them and drops them.

All the same they are matched to the word peach
and must mean more than she sees. She will post them
unripe, in a tiny envelope
to her eight-year-old class-mates, and write
carefully in the ruled-up spaces:
'Where we are the place is a palace.'

An ecstatic preacher

He brought sermons –
frictions of air and breath
blithely pursuing song
in the dust of a hedge bottom.

In Germany the preacher ate Himmel und Erde
beside a river brimming with winter
then bowed down to Bavarian Calvaries,
the dancing of angels
ashed to the point of a pin.

The green river flooded at Innsbruck.
The water touched the feet of the preacher.
He wore dark suits, the good man,
and drank milk in the evenings, cow-warm,
and prayed to the Virgin
of black wood, thumbed over with kisses,
and prayed for the rare feast-day
when milk drops spring from her breasts, and spray
hazes her blue dress.

A meditation on the glasshouses

The bald glasshouses stretch here for miles.
For miles air-vents open like wings.

This is the land of reflections, of heat
flagging from mirror to mirror. Here cloches
force on the fruit by weeks, while pulses
of light run down the chain of glasshouses
and blind the visitors this Good Friday.

The daffodil pickers are spring-white.
Their neat heads in a fuzz of sun
stoop to the buds, make leafless
bunches of ten for Easter.

A white thumb touches the peat
but makes no print. This is the soil-less
Eden of glasshouses, heat-stunned.

The haunting of Epworth

Epworth Rectory was the childhood home of John Wesley. In December 1716 the house was possessed by a poltergeist; after many unsuccessful attempts at exorcism the spirit, nicknamed 'Old Jeffery' by the little Wesley girls, left of its own accord.

Old Jeffery begins his night music.
The girls, sheathed in their brick skin,
giggle with terror. The boys are all gone
out to the world, 'continually sinning',
their graces exotic and paid for.

Old Jeffery rummages pitchforks
up the back chimney. The girls
open the doors to troops of exorcists
who plod back over the Isle of Axeholme
balked by the house. The scrimmage
of iron, shattering windows, and brickwork
chipped away daily is birdsong
morning and evening, or sunlight
into their unsunned lives.

Old Jeffery tires of the house slowly.
He knocks the back of the connubial bed
where nineteen Wesleys, engendered in artlessness
swarm, little ghosts of themselves.
The girls learn to whistle his music.

The house bangs like a side-drum
as Old Jeffery goes out of it. Daughters
in white wrappers mount to the windows, sons
coming from school make notes – the wildness
goes out towards Epworth and leaves nothing
but the bald house straining on tiptoe
after its ghost.

Preaching at Gwennap

Gwennap Pit is a natural amphitheatre in Cornwall, where John Wesley preached.

Preaching at Gwennap, silk
ribbons unrolling far off,
the unteachable turquoise and green
coast dropping far off,

preaching at Gwennap, where thermals revolve
to the bare lip, where granite
breaks its uneasy backbone,
where a great natural theatre, cut
to a hairsbreadth, sends back each cadence,

preaching at Gwennap to a child asleep
while the wide plain murmurs, and prayers
ply on the void, tendered like cords
over the pit's brim.
                                        Off to one side
a horse itches and dreams. Its saddle
comes open, stitch after stitch,

while the tired horse, standing for hours
flicks flies from its arse
and eats through the transfiguration –
old sobersides
mildly eschewing more light.

On circuit from Heptonstall Chapel

''Tis not everyone could bear these things, but I bless God, my wife is less concerned with suffering them than I in writing them.'
(Samuel Wesley, father of John Wesley,
writing of his wife Susanna.)

The mare with her short legs heavily mud-caked
plods, her head down
over the unearthly grasses,
the burning salt-marshes,

through sharp-sided marram and mace
with the rim of the tide's eyelid
out to the right.

The reed-cutters go home
whistling sharply, crab-wise
beneath their dense burdens,

the man on the mare weighs heavy, his broadcloth
shiny and worn, his boots dangling
six inches from ground.
He clenches his buttocks to ease them,
shifts Bible and meat,

thinks of the congregation
gathered beyond town,
wind-whipped, looking for warm
words from his dazed lips.

No brand from the burning;
a thick man with a day's travel
caked on him like salt,

a preacher, one of those scattered like thistle
from the many-angled home chapel
facing all ways on its slabbed upland.

US 1st Division Airborne Ranger at rest in Honduras

The long arm hangs flat to his lap.
The relaxed wrist-joint is tender, shade-
cupped at the base of the thumb.

That long, drab line of American cloth,
those flat brows knitting a crux,
the close-shaven scalp, cheeks, jawbone and lips

rest in abeyance here, solid impermanence
like the stopped breath of a runner swathed up
in tinfoil bodybag, back from the front.

He rests, coloured like August foliage and earth
when the wheat's cropped, and the massive harvesters
go out on hire elsewhere,

his single-lens perspex eyeshield pushed up, denting
the folds of his skull stubble, his cap
shading his eyes which are already shaded
by bone. His pupils are shuttered,
the lenses widening inwards,
notions of a paling behind them.

One more for the beautiful table

Dense slabs of braided-up lupins –
someone's embroidery – Nan,
liking the blue,

one more for the beautiful table
with roses and handkerchiefs, seams
on the web of fifty five-year-olds' life-spans.

New, tough little stitches
run on the torn
wedding head-dresses.
No one can count them
back to the far-off
ghosts of the children's conceptions.

Those party days:

one more for the beautiful table

the extinction of breath in a sash.

What looks and surprises!
Nan on her bad legs
resumes the filminess of petals
and quotes blood pricks and blood stains

faded to mauve and to white and to crisp
brown drifts beneath bare sepals –

look, they have washed out.

Lambkin

A poem in mother dialect

That's better, he says, he says
that's better.

Dense slabs of braided-up lupins –
someone's embroidery – Nan,
liking the blue,

Oh you're a tinker, that's what you are,
a little tinker, a tinker, that's what you are.

One more for the beautiful table
with roses and handkerchiefs, seams
on the web of fifty five-year-olds' life-spans.

Come on now, come on, come on now,
come on, come on, come on now,

new tough little stitches
run on the torn
wedding head-dresses.
The children count them
back to the far-off
ghosts of their own conceptions.

Oh you like that, I know, yes,
you kick those legs, you kick them,
you kick those fat legs then.

Those party days

one more for the beautiful table

set out in the hall.

You mustn't have any tears, you're my good boy
aren't you my little good boy.

What looks and surprises!
Nan on her bad legs
resumes the filminess of petals,

she'll leave it to Carlie
her bad spice.

Let's wipe those tears, let's wipe off all those tears.
That's better, he says, he says
that's right.

She quotes blood pricks and bloodstains
faded to mauve and to white and to crisp
brown drifts beneath bare sepals –

look, they have washed out.

The green recording light falters
as if picking up voices

it's pure noise grain and nothing more human.
It's all right lambkin I've got you I've got you.

In Empire

My daughter Sally moved in Empire seven years ago. That was before people became desperate to get in. Her husband Baines was a prudent man. Sally used to come and visit me regularly, even though I was living out there, and most people in Empire would not do that. I was still in the same house that Sally had grown up in. It was in what we used to call a good neighbourhood, but whatever the goodness was, it was shrinking like a puddle in the sun. Once I'd known almost everyone in the surrounding roads and crescents and avenues, by sight at least, if not to talk to. Sally had grown up with their children. We'd invite each other in at Christmas-time.

Suddenly it seemed that all those people were not there any more. The FOR SALE boards had been stuck in every garden for months, but it was no use: you couldn't sell them. There were people waiting to move in without buying. There was noise on the streets, loud noise. People crying, heels going by fast, fights. There were piles of rubbish under the privet, which grew out of shape, tall and flowering.

Baines began to tell Sally that it was too risky for her to drive over with the children, even though of course they had Armaflex on the car by then. But Sally did come, first once a week, then twice a month, then less often.

One Sunday they all came over together. It was a hot, cloudy, close day, and I had put the paddling pool out in the garden for Mel and Royston, but Baines would not let them go out of the house. Kidnapping had started, although so far only in London and the big cities. Sally was tired out, and the children were restless, irritable, impossible to amuse. It was a relief when they went, and I could start clearing up the mess from the spoilt day we'd all had.

Baines telephoned me later. Sally was in bed, she had been sick. Luckily the children had fallen asleep almost as soon as they drove off, so they hadn't seen anything.

Of course nobody would ever stop on the journey between our district and Empire. Baines took one of the stretches of motorway which was still passable. It would bring him within a mile of Empire. But as he slowed down on the slip road off the motorway, he saw a bundle of people step out from the banks and fan all over the road. He didn't stop, but he slowed. He couldn't help it, he said, it was pure reaction. The tyres were Armaflexed, so he wasn't too worried. He had spent a lot of money on that Venturer.

Sally shrank back in her seat, because you can't help doing that when those faces moon up to you against the windows, laughing at you. Baines kept moving through, nudging his way, not looking to either side. He was trying to think what he'd do if there was another ambush up ahead. Baines did not tell me much about what happened next, but Sally told me, a few days later, when I was helping her to stake delphiniums in the long herbaceous border in Empire. They prize such borders in Empire. I have always loved them myself, though they went out of fashion for many years. They were too labour-intensive. But that doesn't matter now. We watch the accredited daily workers move up and down, sober and skilful, glad to be safely within Empire. They have to go out there at night, of course. Sally likes to do a bit of gardening. It helps her to relax.

She told me that there was a girl of about twenty, with fleecy, glistening blonde hair, like a child's hair. She was in front of their car, just standing there as it came on towards her. She had a baby in her arms, a little one, not more than two months, Sally thought. Sally is still at the stage where she can tell babies' ages to the month. She speaks the mother dialect. The girl smiled at Sally, then she put the baby down in the path of the car, and stepped neatly aside. She skipped, almost, Sally said.

Baines drove over it. Well, Sally said that the wheels couldn't have gone over the baby, not the wheels themselves. Baines zigzagged a little, as much as was safe, so that the car would go over the baby, but not the wheels. Or so she said. Anyway, the baby disappeared, and as they drove forward the knot of people in front and to the side of them melted away as they ran around to the back of the Venturer to see what had become of the baby.

It eased my mind a little when Sally told me that they had done that. At least they had not thought of anything else but their baby. But what will they think of next time?

Baines accelerated, got off the slip road and safely into Empire, with the children still sleeping in the back.

After that he wouldn't let Sally come at all. A few months later they found me a place in Empire. I do the babysitting patrol, ten p.m. until 6 a.m. I am armed, in spite of the perimeter shock section and the guard towers. In return for this I have a small room, a semi-basement, but it looks out over the garden. It was only because of Baines and Sally that I got the room at all, since everyone wants to be in Empire now, and unless you've got something serious to offer, there is no chance.

I help Sally with the children when she has finished work, and I like to work in the garden, especially in the herbaceous borders. The best time is very early in the morning, after I finish my patrol, but before the accredited workers are allowed in. I don't need much sleep. I have got to know the plants well. I look out for anything new: a variegation of colour or shading. It doesn't often occur with perennials, but sometimes I find a plant which I can breed from. Sally doesn't like the way I try to develop these sports. She likes the generations to breed true, parent to child, parent to child, replicating themselves. It's understandable, I suppose.

Dublin 1971

The grass looks different in another country.
By a shade more or a shade less, it startles
as love does in the sharply-tinged landscape
of sixteen to eighteen. When it is burnt
midsummer and lovers have learned to make love
with scarcely a word said, then they see nothing
but what is closest: an eyelash tonight,
the slow spread of a sweat stain,
the shoe-sole of the other as he walks off
watched from the mattress.

The top deck of the bus babbles with diplomats'
children returning from school, their language
an overcast August sky which can't clear.
Each syllable melting to static
troubles the ears of strangers, no stranger
but less sure than the slick-limbed children.
With one silvery, tarnishing ring between them
they walk barefoot past the Martello tower
at Sandymount, and wish the sea clearer,
the sun for once dazzling, fledged
from its wet summer nest of cloud-strips.

They make cakes of apple peel and arrowroot
and hear the shrieks of bold, bad seven-year-old Seamus
who holds the pavement till gone midnight
for all his mother's forlorn calling.
The freedom of no one related for thousands of miles,
the ferry forever going backward and forward
from rain runnel to drain cover...

The grass looks different in another country,
sudden and fresh, waving, unfurling
the last morning they see it, as they go down
to grey Dun Laoghaire by taxi.
They watch the slate rain coming in eastward
pleating the sea not swum in,
blotting the Ballsbridge house with its soft sheets
put out in the air to sweeten.

The hard-hearted husband

'Has she gone then?' they asked,
stepping round the back of the house
whose cat skulked in the grass.

She'd left pegs dropped in the bean-row,
and a mauve terrycloth babygrow
stirred on the line as I passed.

Her damsons were ripe and her sage was in flower,
her roses tilted from last night's downpour,
her sweetpeas and sunflowers leaned anywhere.

'She got sick of it, then,' they guessed,
and wondered if the torn-up paper
might be worth reading, might be a letter.

'It was the bills got her,' they knew,
seeing brown envelopes sheafed with the white
in a jar on the curtainless windowsill,

some of them sealed still, as if she was through
with trying to pay, and would sit, chilled,
ruffling and arranging them like flowers
in the long dusks while the kids slept upstairs.

The plaster was thick with her shadows,
damp and ready to show
how she lived there and lay fallow

and how she stood at her window
and watched tall pylons stride down the slope
sizzling faintly, stepping away
as she now suddenly goes,

too stubborn to be ghosted at thirty.
She will not haunt here. She picks up her dirty
warm children and takes them

down to the gate which she lifts as it whines
and sets going a thin cry in her.
He was hard-hearted and no good to her
they say now, grasping the chance to be kind.

The old friends

After the welcome, the facts.
Your children who are no longer children
ignore us. They push through the kitchen,
their tight-jeaned buttocks butting our chair-backs,

and your ten-year-old daughter's turned ugly. Rat-fair,
watching you, Daddy, she uses long words
where short ones would do, wishes that we were not here –
she'll read too many books, haunt libraries, suffer…

I go out to look at your garden
and watch your hands move among leaves,
tinkering, clearing off weeds.
You speak of it as you spoke of the children
years back: a luminous burden

tying you, tiding you over
the numb years of your mid-forties.
Your job marks time, and the bliss
of casual motherhood's gone altogether.

You see us off at the lane-end, sun in the frown
gilding your face. The children are nowhere.
No matter how long I crane backward, or peer
at the dark hedge where your coat's brown
against brown, your face white as the frost,
I catch nothing of you.

At Wall-town Crags

Four fifty-year-old Americans patrol the wall.
Two women in trouser-suits, slack-buttocked, intimate,
smile at strangers after their farm breakfast
while two men josh as they load up more film.

Myrtle and Claud are insiders, fresh
from the bright stores and quarters at Lakenheath
where their boy Calvin and all the fine
young men lounge, loose-limbed with readiness.

At Housesteads they trace grainstores
and put bare fingers in carving –
graffiti of debts, likelihoods, postings,
solid to the palm as plums.
They edge sideways, rustling translations.

'Must've been cold for them here.'
'Feels kind of dark, too.' No chance to stand up
sharp as a pin and be counted miles off.

Thin wind combs down a tarn.
They hear the ringing of masts at Mystic,
they see the red stems of the dogwood
pattern the sides of white houses.

A legion got lost in the drizzle
at fifty paces, but you could still feel its
boot-throbs diffuse through the bog-cotton.
Arnie soothes his friend down. The light's useless.
They'll fix the lens cap, spend time with the girls.

Myrtle and Alice lean forward, soft-rumped
over the camp plan, murmuring mild
gobbets of fact. In name only, they're wild
for Q Florus Maternus. They too push coins in
shrines and make their local dedications.

They spread out a Black Watch blanket
in the least damp spot. When the ground quakes
from old disturbances, locked miles down,
they shake out dry picnic crumbs.

Myrtle and Alice lower themselves slowly.
Mute, stone-walled fields slide
under a sunless, quick-moving sky –
a quenched landscape, soaked till it sucks
their careless fingers, trailed off the rug.
Brigantia perhaps
fusing with Mithras, smiles from the shrines
which thank and beseech luck.

When they got to the camp it was dark
and as they slowed for the guard
little blowing lamps flocked to their coach
so Myrtle nearly cried out, though Claud said it was best
to look elsewhere. Calvin had written them
'Act like you don't see anything.'

A clot of bodies, faces turned up whitely,
with round dark mouths moving in them. She guessed
some would be women. They might have been singing
but the coach's sound system drowned them.

Later, when they were within,
touring the squash courts and cinema
Cal said, 'Don't judge the country
by them. Wait'll you meet Lisa!'

Four fifty-year-old Americans patrol the Wall.
Myrtle and Arnie, Alice and Claud,
out of their couples whose flesh made
Calvin and all the fine boys.
They've checked out Housesteads, Corstopitum,
and now at Wall-town Crags they're alone
sounding the air with long vowels.
Even when they think it's still
they feel some wind troubling the harebells,
and Claud looks sideways, seeing despite himself
the bulge where Alice's corset digs in
her soft flesh and hampers her smiles.

St Bonaventure's in a snowstorm

A cold morning, dusky with falling snow.
I come into the porch
and shut the mirror-glazed doors quickly.
The church air, in its casing of stone
stays warm. Today there's the rare
blizzard of Bristol winters: one in five years
elating and fierce as this.

A weekday Mass, with twenty or thirty
packed into balaclavas and scarves. Only a slip
of each face shows, lips moving, eyes closed.
Snow clods unfuse slowly, and drops gather.

The church that was green and crimson
and swagged with garlands for Christmas
is plain now, sunk back
onto the bare pulse of the Mass.

Light backs on itself, fans upward
from earth to the thick sky.
It stops at the stained-glass windows
and leaves them solid as paint blocks.

A pair of stiff little altar boys
walks up and down. The heat-loving cat
stirs on her shelf, yawns, gleams
round with her green glances.

When I come out the snow's dizzying,
vivid with colour, as if each particle
shaken, gives off crimson and green
to where I stand at the base
of down-funnelling snowflakes.

But I adjust from the church dark
into the city landscape beaten to white
sheets, jewel-like sheathed
stems bursting from snow-crusts

for half a morning and then thaw blurs it.
A lorry, its diesel unwaxed,
thrashes through slush, unevenly loaded
with frozen, opaque purple and green cabbages.

Malta

The sea's a featureless blaze.
On photographs nothing comes out
but glare, with that scarlet-rimmed fishing boat
far-off, lost to the lens.

At noon a stiff-legged tourist in shorts
steps, camera poised. He's stilted
as a flamingo, pink-limbed.

Icons of Malta gather around him.
He sweats as a procession passes
and women with church-dark faces
brush him as if he were air.

He holds a white crocheted dress
to give to his twelve-year-old daughter
who moons in the apartment, sun-sore.
The sky's tight as a drum, hard
to breathe in, hard to walk under.

He would not buy 'bikini for daughter'
though the man pressed him, with plump fingers
spreading out scraps of blue cotton.

Let her stay young, let her know nothing.
Let her body remain skimpy and sudden.
His wife builds arches of silence over her
new breasts and packets of tampons marked 'slender'.
At nights, when they think she's asleep,
they ache in the same places
but never louder than in a whisper.

He watches more women melt into a porch.
Their white, still laundry flags from window to window
while they are absent, their balconies blank.

At six o'clock, when he comes home and snicks
his key in the lock so softly neither will catch it
he hears one of them laugh.
They are secret in the kitchen, talking of nothing,
strangers whom anyone might love.

Candlemas

Snowdrops, Mary's tapers,
barely alight in the grey shadows,

Candlemas in a wet February,
the soil clodded and frostless,
the quick blue shadows of snowlight again missed.

The church candles' mass
yellow as mothering bee cells,
melts to soft puddles of wax,

the snowdrops, with crisp ruffs
and green spikes clearing the leaf debris

are an unseen nebula
caught by a swinging telescope,

white tapers
blooming in structureless dusk.

Pilgrims

Let us think that we are pilgrims
in furs on this bleak water.
The Titanic's lamps hang on its sides like fruit
on lit cliffs. We're shriven for rescue.

The sea snaps at our caulking.
We bend to our oars and praise God
and flex our fingers to bring
a drowned child out from the tarpaulin.

We're neither mothers nor fathers, but children,
fearful and full of trust,
lamblike as the Titanic goes down
entombing its witnesses.

We row on in a state of grace
in our half-empty lifeboats, sailing
westward for America, pilgrims,
numb to the summer-like choir
of fifteen hundred companions.

An Irish miner in Staffordshire

On smooth buttercup fields
the potholers sink down like dreams
close to Roman lead-mining country.

I sink the leafless shaft of an hydrangea twig
down through the slippy spaces I've made for it.
Dusted with hormone powder, moist,
its fibrous stem splays into root.

I graze the soft touches of compost
and wash them off easily, balled
under the thumb – clean dirt.
There's the man who gave me my Irish name

still going down, wifeless, that miner
who shafted the narrow cuffs of the earth
as if it was this he came for.